HOWARD BRENTON

Howard Brenton was born in Portsmouth in 1942. His many
plays include *Christie in Love* (Portable Theatre, 1969); *Revenge*
(Theatre Upstairs, 1969); *Magnificence* (Royal Court Theatre,
1973); *The Churchill Play* (Nottingham Playhouse, 1974, and
twice revived by the RSC, 1978 and 1988); *Bloody Poetry* (Foco
Novo, 1984, and Royal Court Theatre, 1987); *Weapons of
Happiness* (National Theatre, Evening Standard Award, 1976);
Epsom Downs (Joint Stock Theatre, 1977); *Sore Throats* (RSC,
1978); *The Romans in Britain* (National Theatre, 1980, revived
at the Crucible Theatre, Sheffield, 2006); *Thirteenth Night* (RSC,
1981); *The Genius* (1983), *Greenland* (1988) and *Berlin Bertie*
(1992), all presented by the Royal Court; *Kit's Play* (RADA
Jerwood Theatre, 2000); *Paul* (National Theatre, 2005); *In
Extremis* (Shakespeare's Globe, 2006 and 2007); *Never So Good*
(National Theatre, 2008); *The Ragged Trousered Philanthropists*
adapted from the novel by Robert Tressell (Liverpool Everyman
and Chichester Festival Theatre, 2010); *Anne Boleyn*
(Shakespeare's Globe, 2010 and 2011); *55 Days* (Hampstead
Theatre, 2012); *#aiww: The Arrest of Ai Weiwei* (Hampstead
Theatre, 2013), *The Guffin* (NT Connections, 2013) and
Drawing the Line (Hampstead Theatre, 2013).

Collaborations with other writers include *Brassneck* (with David
Hare, Nottingham Playhouse, 1972); *Pravda* (with David Hare,
National Theatre, Evening Standard Award, 1985) and *Moscow
Gold* (with Tariq Ali, RSC, 1990).

Versions of classics include *The Life of Galileo* (1980) and
Danton's Death (1982) both for the National Theatre, Goethe's
Faust (1995/6) for the RSC, a new version of *Danton's Death*
for the National Theatre (2010) and *Dances of Death* (Gate
Theatre, 2013).

He wrote thirteen episodes of the BBC1 drama series *Spooks*
(2001–05, BAFTA Best Drama Series, 2003).

Howard Brenton

ETERNAL LOVE

The Story of Abelard and Heloise

NICK HERN BOOKS
London
www.nickhernbooks.co.uk

A Nick Hern Book

Eternal Love first published in Great Britain as a paperback original in 2014 by Nick Hern Books Limited, The Glasshouse, 49a Goldhawk Road, London W12 8QP

Originally published as *In Extremis* in 2006

Eternal Love copyright © 2006, 2014 Howard Brenton

Howard Brenton has asserted his right to be identified as the author of this work

Cover image: Robert Day
Cover design: Ned Hoste, 2H

Typeset by Nick Hern Books, London
Printed in the UK by Mimeo Ltd, Huntingdon, Cambridgeshire PE29 6XX

A CIP catalogue record for this book is available from the British Library

ISBN 978 1 84842 384 8

Eternal Love was first produced and performed by English
Touring Theatre on 6 February 2014 at Cambridge Arts Theatre,
before touring the UK. The cast was as follows:

ABELARD	David Sturzaker
HELOISE	Jo Herbert
BERNARD OF CLAIRVAUX	Sam Crane
FULBERT/BISHOP	Edward Peel
DENISE/NUN	Rhiannon Oliver
WILLIAM OF CHAMPEAUX/ COUSIN 1	Tim Frances
LOUIS VI	Julius D'Silva
ALBERIC	John Cummins
LOTHOLF	William Mannering
HELENE/WORKING WOMAN	Sally Edwards
BERTHODE	Holly Morgan
MARIE	Daisy Hughes
FRANCINE	Claire Bond
COUSIN 2	Tom Kanji
STUDENT 1	Robert Heard
STUDENT 2	Kevin Leslie
STUDENT 3	Sid Sagar
MUSICIANS	William Lyons (MD), Rebecca Austen-Brown, Arngeir Hauksson

All other parts played by members of the company

Director	John Dove
Designer	Michael Taylor
Lighting Designer	Paul Russell
Sound Designer	Derrick Zieba
Composer	William Lyons
Casting Director	Matilda James
Choreographer	Sian Williams
Assistant Director	Joshua Roche

The play was orginally performed as *In Extremis* at
Shakespeare's Globe, London, on 27 August 2006 and revived
there on 15 May 2007. The cast was as follows:

ABELARD	Oliver Boot
HELOISE	Sally Bretton
BERNARD OF CLAIRVAUX	Jack Laskey
FULBERT	Fred Ridgeway
DENISE	Pascale Burgess
WILLIAM OF CHAMPEAUX	John Bett
LOUIS VI	Colin Hurley
ALBERIC	Patrick Brennan
LOTHOLF	William Mannering
HELENE/WOMAN 1	Sheila Reid
BERTHODE/NUN/WOMAN	Frances Thorburn
MARIE/COURTIER/ WHORE/NUN	Niamh McCann
FRANCINE/WOMAN 2/ COURTIER/NUN	Rhiannon Oliver
FULBERT'S COUSINS/ STUDENTS/COURTIERS/ MONKS/DRUNKEN BISHOPS/MAD MONKS	Tas Emiabata, David Hinton, Simon Muller, Paul Lloyd, Tom Stuart

Director	John Dove
Designer	Michael Taylor
Choreographer	Sian Williams
Composer/Arranger	William Lyons

8

Characters

ABELARD
HELOISE
BERNARD OF CLAIRVAUX
FULBERT
DENISE
WILLIAM OF CHAMPEAUX
LOUIS VI
ALBERIC
LOTHOLF
HELENE
BERTHODE
FRANCINE
FULBERT'S COUSINS
STUDENTS
COURTIERS
MONKS
DRUNKEN BISHOPS
MAD MONKS

ACT ONE

Scene One

Cloisters.

HELOISE *and* WOMEN FRIENDS *are leaving church with* FULBERT, *Heloise's uncle. He is a canon. When the young* WOMEN *are in his sight, they are demure. When he looks away, they hit each other playfully behind his back. He never quite catches them.*

FULBERT. I have always known I would never be great.

HELOISE. No, Uncle. I mean yes, Uncle.

FULBERT. But I look at our city of Paris shining in God's light this Trinity Sunday morning...

He indicates the landscape and looks away. HELOISE *and her* FRIENDS *hit each other.*

...and when I look up at our great church of Notre Dame...

He turns, they stop hitting each other.

I know that I am at least near to greatness.

HELOISE. You are a canon of the great church, Uncle. St Augustine teaches us that to be part of the City of God is to be part of greatness.

FULBERT. Ah, Heloise. Have you actually *read* St Augustine's *City of God*?

HELOISE. Yes, Uncle.

FULBERT. It is a book of such vast dimensions, I am amazed a girl of seventeen can lift it, let alone read it.

HELOISE. Oh, I can't lift it, Uncle.

FULBERT. My dear, your cleverness is a wonder and a pleasure to me.

HELOISE *bows. Her* FRIENDS *look down. He turns away, they start hitting each other again.*

Is our Paris the new Jerusalem on earth, built by the power of learning? And the power of the wool trade of course. Wool and theology.

He turns. They stop. A pause. Does he suspect something?

Perhaps there is a sermon for me to give in there.

HELOISE. Shall I write it for you, Uncle? It will be on the sanctity of sheep, and the shearing of St Augustine.

FULBERT. Was St Augustine sheared?

HELOISE. As a young heathen, by the knife of God's grace.

FULBERT. Is God's grace a knife?

HELOISE. Yes, it cuts our conscience.

FULBERT. Mm. (*Pauses, eyeing the precocious* HELOISE.) Write it rough. I will smooth it with a man's hand.

WILLIAM OF CHAMPEAUX *enters, with young* MEN *and* MONKS, *amongst them* ALBERIC, LOTHOLF *and* PETER ABELARD.

FRANCINE. It's the cloister school!

MARIE. What are they saying?

WILLIAM (*droning*). Therefore, as Plato has taught us, there is, in Heaven, the perfect form of everything that is in this world.

HELOISE. I think he's teaching Plato's universals.

MARIE. Oh dear.

HELOISE. It's what Magister William is famous for. Plato's theory that everything on earth is only a copy of what is in Heaven.

MARIE. Right.

HELOISE *steps forward to listen.*

WILLIAM. A carpenter makes a table, badly.

STUDENT. It's got three legs.

All but ABELARD *laugh.* WILLIAM *is irritated.*

WILLIAM. But though a table upon earth be imperfect, in Heaven there is the perfect table. The abstract table, the form to which all earthly tables aspire. It is the universal idea of a table, in the mind of God.

ABELARD. I disagree.

FRANCINE. Who... is... that?

WILLIAM *shudders*. ALBERIC *and* LOTHOLF *are disgusted. The other* STUDENTS *are excited.*

WILLIAM. Not again, Abelard, I beg you.

ABELARD. Magister, tell me, this piece of ideal furniture, around which the saints in Heaven sit for their dinner...

A suppressed giggle from a STUDENT.

...does it have four sides?

WILLIAM. It's a table. Yes yes.

ABELARD. And four legs?

WILLIAM (*a moment's hesitation*). Yes yes.

ABELARD (*points at a* STUDENT). Is your table with *three* legs a good table?

STUDENT 1. It could be like a big stool.

STUDENT 2. A tripod. Like they have for the big candles, at the high altar...

STUDENT 3. And round.

ABELARD. Why not?

WILLIAM. Ah...

ABELARD (*ignoring* WILLIAM, *concentrating on the* STUDENTS). And would this round, three-legged table, work for the less than ideal dinners we eat on earth?

STUDENT 2. Why not?

ABELARD (*to* WILLIAM). Then would we not have a perfection on earth, which does not follow its perfection in Heaven?

WILLIAM. No no. You would have an inadequacy on earth. No matter how many meals you eat off it, it will forever be a shadow of the perfection in Heaven.

ABELARD. But this perfection in Heaven... You've told us it has four legs and four sides.

WILLIAM. Yes.

ABELARD. How long is it? How wide?

WILLIAM. It's long and wide enough. Because it's perfect.

ABELARD. But perfect for what? For a father and mother and son to have a meal? Perfect for ten to have a meal? Perfect for five thousand? And if the archangels in Heaven themselves are huge beings, as some say they are, is the table big enough for them to sit at? Magister William, please tell us, exactly how long, exactly how wide, how tall, how thick, how shiny, how rough is this perfect table? And if any table on earth is a near imperfect copy, does that mean that the heavenly table is wider, taller, thicker, shinier, rougher than any on earth? No, surely, if a stool or a flat stone is good enough to eat bread from, it's as good a table as any other. The essence of the table is not its heavenly perfection. Its essence is its function, here on earth.

All look at WILLIAM, *who is taking short breaths and for a moment cannot speak.*

WILLIAM. Day after day I have this from you. Stop it! Just stop it!

ABELARD. I am disputing.

WILLIAM. There is nothing to dispute. I am the teacher, you are the student. I teach, you learn and that is that.

ABELARD. But, Magister, how can I know that what you teach is true, unless I question it? And, if my reasoning is right, that the essence of things is their function on earth, must we not conclude that the whole idea of heavenly forms, of universals, is nonsense?

WILLIAM (*losing it.* ALBERIC *and* LOTHOLF *support him*). How dare you.

HELOISE *raises a hand, as if to ask a question herself.*
ABELARD *sees her. They stare at each other.*

ALBERIC. To question the universals is to question the Trinity itself.

Some of the STUDENTS *look shocked.*

FULBERT (*to* HELOISE *and her* FRIENDS). I think we should withdraw. Philosophy can be dangerous to ignorant ears.

HELOISE. Not ignorant, just innocent.

FULBERT. Heloise! Enough.

She turns away. She takes a look back at ABELARD.
They exit.

LOTHOLF. Yes. If there is no universal spirit, how can Father, Son and Holy Ghost be one and the same?

ALBERIC. A nasty little heresy, a weed growing in your logic, Peter Abelard.

ABELARD. Down, dogs. You aren't arguing, you're barking.

The STUDENTS *laugh.*

Magister.

WILLIAM (*weak*). What?

ABELARD. Tell me why I am wrong.

WILLIAM (*a pause*). I can't.

The STUDENTS *are amazed.*

I must rest now.

ABELARD. It is a matter of words, Magister. The logic of words. If we cannot speak logically about silly tables, how will we ever be able to speak of God?

WILLIAM. Please, why do you have to speak so loudly so everyone can hear?

ABELARD. So everyone can hear I'm right!

Laughter amongst the STUDENTS.

WILLIAM. This new philosophy, this new logic. Young men questioning, I can no longer... I...

He exits, helped by ALBERIC *and* LOTHOLF. *The other* STUDENTS *wait respectfully, then when he is gone they rush at* ABELARD *and embrace him. They fall on the ground in a heap, laughing.*

STUDENT 1. You've done for him, Peter. Set up your own school! We'll be your first students.

STUDENT 2. They'll come from all over France, when they know the new learning is being taught. Disputation!

STUDENT 3. Disputation! Argument! Aristotle!

ABELARD *takes* STUDENT 4 *aside.*

ABELARD. That girl. I want her.

Scene Two

FULBERT*'s house.*

ABELARD, HELOISE *with a book, and* FULBERT. HELOISE *stands apart. She and* ABELARD *do not look at each other.*

FULBERT. My girl, a student of Peter Abelard? I am overwhelmed. That you would take time away from your new school, to teach a woman privately, such generosity! I will be in your debt, Magister. (*Bows.*)

ABELARD. I have heard she is a great reader, with a quick mind, I thought it my duty to offer instruction.

FULBERT. But you don't think it unnatural, such learning in a woman?

ABELARD. It is a gift of God, to the world.

FULBERT. Yes! Yes! And in my family! (*More intimate with* ABELARD.) She is my niece, but in my heart, she is my daughter. She was all but a beggar when they found her, an orphan, living in the ruin of my brother's farm, burnt by Breton bandits. We had given her up for dead, or captured by those animals. But she'd hidden herself, eating what she could from the orchards, the fruits of brambles… Now my little wild animal eats books. (*Turns to her.*) Don't you, my dear! You eat a book by St Jerome for breakfast!

She bows, remaining silent. ABELARD *and she still do not look at each other. A pause.*

So, when do you want…

ABELARD. Now.

FULBERT. Begin now? Why not? Do you wish to withdraw somewhere private?

ABELARD. Absolute privacy is essential. No interruptions.

FULBERT. Everyone in the household will be told. No one will come near this part of the house. This room is quiet, a window overlooking the garden. Perhaps here?

Scene Three

A room in FULBERT*'s house.*

ABELARD *and* HELOISE. *She still holds a book. They stand within touching distance.*

For the first time they look at each other.

ABELARD. So you were found on your family's farm, running wild?

HELOISE. No.

ABELARD. Then why does your uncle say that you were?

HELOISE. He likes to tell that story about me.

ABELARD. But people only have to ask you if it's true.

HELOISE. They don't.

    A pause.

ABELARD. So what is the story of your childhood?

HELOISE. I don't care. Why should you? All that matters is we wake up each morning and find ourselves still on our journey.

ABELARD (*suspecting, wrongly, that this is a platitude*). Yes, our journey to God.

HELOISE. Or our journey to…

A silence. Her words hang between them. ABELARD *breaks first.*

ABELARD. So you read a lot.

HELOISE. It's not what you read, it's how you read, don't you think?

ABELARD. And how –

HELOISE (*interrupting*). As a woman.

ABELARD. The womanly way of reading being –

HELOISE. Oh, to seek in the familiar, what is hidden.

A silence.

ABELARD. What book do you have there?

HELOISE. St Jerome's *Against Jovinian*.

ABELARD. With its warning against sensual, earthly love.

HELOISE. Yes.

ABELARD. And what is hidden there? That a woman can find?

HELOISE *just looks at him.*

Shall we read it? Or eat it for breakfast?

They smile. A pause. He gestures to her. She reads.

HELOISE. 'The senses are like windows through which the vices gain entry into the soul.

He holds out his hand and touches her eyes and her face.

She is still.

A silence.

He lowers his hand. She reads on.

'If… if anyone takes pleasure in the circus, and athletic contests, an actor's pantomime or a woman's beauty, the splendour of jewels and garments or anything of that sort… the liberty of his soul is captured through the eye.'

*Now she puts out her hand and touches his eyes and his face.
She lowers her hand.*

Shall I read the next sentence?

ABELARD. We both know it by heart.

HELOISE (*looking directly at him*). 'The liberty of his soul
is captured through the eye, and the word of the prophet
is fulfilled...

ABELARD *and* HELOISE. 'Death has climbed in through our
windows.'

*He takes the book from her, holds it to his mouth and bites
a page.*

*She joins him – they're both biting the book. They wrestle,
the book held in their mouths. They break away, the book
falls to the floor. They talk fast.*

ABELARD. Will your father...?

HELOISE. Uncle not my father.

ABELARD. Uncle.

HELOISE. No he won't listen. He respects you.

ABELARD. Who, below the window...

HELOISE. It's vegetables. The gardener is deaf.

ABELARD. Are you sure?

HELOISE. Yes, deaf gardener.

A pause.

ABELARD. In this room, in what is about to happen...
(*A pause.*) You may be as much teacher as I.

HELOISE. I have read Ovid, *The Arts of Love*. But now, I think,
we are not going to read, we are going to do.

*A moment's pause. They begin to move toward each other
to embrace.*

Scene Four

Fields outside the city.

WOMEN *working.*

ALBERIC *and* LOTHOLF *enter,* LOTHOLF *carrying a half-paralysed* WILLIAM *on his back. They set* WILLIAM *down upon the ground. Saliva runs from his mouth.*

A distance away, two WOMEN *are working in the fields, very slowly.*

The three MEN *rest for a while. Then* WILLIAM *is disturbed.*

LOTHOLF. They're coming, Magister. You'll see.

> WILLIAM *tries to speak. It is impossible to make out his words.*

ALBERIC. Yes, in the open air. This is where he teaches.

LOTHOLF. In the fields! Spraying his ideas everywhere, like a tomcat. (*Furious.*) Peasants, splattered by the filthy, stinking cat's spunk of his philosophy! It's wrong!

ALBERIC. Here they come.

WILLIAM. W… W…

ALBERIC. Yes, women too. Not in his new school at Mont Ste Geneviève, of course. Not in the Abbey itself. But when he wanders around, when he becomes 'Peter the Peripatetic', as they call him, all kinds attach themselves.

> ABELARD *enters, striding across the stage at a vigorous speed. He is followed by young* MEN *and* WOMEN, HELOISE *among them.*

ABELARD. Don't think 'yes *or* no', think 'Yes *and* no'.

STUDENT 1. Do you understand that?

STUDENT 2. Yes and no.

> *Laughter.*

ABELARD. What am I talking about?

HELOISE. Dialectic!

STUDENTS (*chanting*). Aristotle, Aristotle, Aristotle…

ABELARD. Thesis, antithesis, synthesis. Dialectic! Do it. (*Points to one of the* WOMEN.) A thesis.

WOMAN. All women are human.

Laughter.

ABELARD. Antithesis.

He points to one of the MEN.

MAN. All men are human.

Laughter.

ABELARD. Synthesis!

ALL. All humans are men and women.

Laughter, which ABELARD *rides over.*

ABELARD. But…

He waits until they are silent.

But, are all the fathers of men, men?

STUDENTS. Yes!

ABELARD. Is God the Father, a man?

A silence.

The STUDENTS *are dismayed.*

HELOISE. Yes, when he is Christ.

ABELARD. See! Logic can approach even the Trinity itself.

He smiles. The STUDENTS *relax and laugh. Leaving* WILLIAM *to lie on a corner of the stage,* ALBERIC *and* LOTHOLF *approach* ABELARD, *smiling. The* STUDENTS *are silent.*

LOTHOLF. Magister, may we bark with you?

A little laughter.

ABELARD. Dear dogs, yes.

ALBERIC. This Aristotle logic. We hear that you use it upon Holy Scripture.

ABELARD. To *understand* Holy Scripture.

ALBERIC. So when our Lord Jesus walked upon the water...

LOTHOLF. St Matthew's Gospel, chapter fourteen, verses twenty-five and twenty-six: 'Between three and six in the morning, Jesus went unto them, walking on the water. And when the disciples saw him walking on the water, they were troubled, saying "It is a ghost"; and they cried out in fear.'

ABELARD. What is your point?

ALBERIC. My *point* is, that we are taught that Christ was the word made flesh. He was the Son of Man. Christ was a man. Men cannot walk upon water. Synthesis: the Scripture is wrong. (*Pauses.*) Is that not logical, Magister?

A silence.

ABELARD. Yes and no. (*Pauses.*) Yes, he walked upon the waters of Galilee because the Scriptures say so. And no he did not, because he was a man come down to us, to lead us upon our journey.

Shock amongst the STUDENTS.

ALBERIC. Confused for a dialectical, logical teacher, Abelard.

ABELARD. Not at all. Logic can only help us approach the mysteries of Scripture. After all, weren't the disciples themselves confused when they saw our Lord, walking across the water toward them? They thought he was a ghost. (*Smiling at his* STUDENTS.) If logic reveals confusion, so be it.

ALBERIC. What if it reveals mystery?

ABELARD. Mystery, confusion, what is the difference? In the end, both will flee before the light of philosophy.

The STUDENTS *enjoy that.*

ALBERIC. Thank you for your instruction, Magister.

He bows.

LOTHOLF. Magister.

ABELARD and his STUDENTS *stride away.*

ABELARD (*to his* STUDENTS). Now! Exercises! Dialectical thinking needs muscles in the mind. I give you this from the divine Aristotle: 'If pleasure is a good thing...'

ALL. 'A bad thing is no pleasure…'

They exit. ALBERIC *and* LOTHOLF *go back to* WILLIAM. *They lift him and begin to make their way off.*

ALBERIC. It's true, Magister, he's letting Aristotle loose on Holy Scripture.

LOTHOLF. He said the Gospel story was confused!

WILLIAM *shakes uncontrollably. He rouses himself with a great effort. He holds onto* ALBERIC *and* LOTHOLF. *He speaks with a great effort.*

WILLIAM. God.

ALBERIC. Magister?

WILLIAM. He – will kill – God.

ALBERIC. Then there's no hope.

WILLIAM. Tell… Bernard… at… Clairvaux.

He loses consciousness.

LOTHOLF (*frightened*). Go to Bernard's monastery? You know what they say about that place.

ALBERIC. We must stop Abelard. Even if we have to go to the ends of the earth.

They carry WILLIAM *off. The* WOMEN *look up from their labours.*

WOMAN 1. Monks everywhere, these days. Scuttling about the fields, like rats.

WOMAN 2. Rat runs, monk runs.

They laugh. ABELARD *and* HELOISE *come on, holding hands.*

WOMAN 1. Those two again. They were in the fish pond round the back of the little wood, yesterday. Naked with the carp.

WOMAN 2. Had his fish up her tail, did he?

WOMAN 1. My son's being taught by monks. He doesn't go nude in fish ponds with girls. He spends all his time on his knees, praying or cleaning the monastery latrines.

WOMAN 2. He's just a peasant boy. Not one of this lot.

They exit.

A moment, then DENISE *enters.*

DENISE. Peter!

ABELARD *and* HELOISE *turn. They are still.*

ABELARD. Denise.

He runs to her, they embrace. HELOISE *hangs back.*

DENISE. You look wonderfully well.

ABELARD. The benefits of open-air teaching.

DENISE (*looking at* HELOISE). And of other things, no doubt, brother dear.

ABELARD. Heloise, this is my sister, Denise.

HELOISE *approaches, then stops.*

DENISE. And you are…

HELOISE. One of your brother's other things.

DENISE. I see.

They look at each other, not knowing whether they will like each other.

HELOISE. I must go. I want to be there when my uncle gets home.

ABELARD. Good.

They hold hands.

This afternoon, above the deaf gardener's vegetables?

HELOISE *looks down, conscious of* DENISE *staring at her. She exits.*

DENISE. She's young.

ABELARD. Yes. How is our father?

DENISE. Well. Complaining about you, in your absence.

ABELARD. And who is our present mother? Is it still the girl who washes out the cheese churns?

DENISE. We are beyond her. Our present mother is the girl who looks after the pigs.

ABELARD. Don't tell me she actually does smell in the house.

DENISE. She is true to her station in life.

ABELARD (*amused*). Father, Father… will he ever rest?

DENISE. He sent me, of course. The news of your school has even reached the coast of Brittany. She's *very* young.

ABELARD. Our pig-girl mother?

DENISE. Don't be obtuse.

ABELARD. It's just lust. We've never had too much trouble enjoying the sins of the flesh in our family, have we, sister dear. He thinks I'm making money, I suppose.

DENISE. Come home.

ABELARD. I can't abandon my students just like that…

DENISE. Come home before it's too late.

ABELARD. What do you mean, before what's too late?

DENISE. Peter, on my way here, I stayed a night with the nuns of the Convent of Ste Marie Argenteuil.

ABELARD. A good house.

DENISE. A gossipy house. At supper, the talk was of nothing but your school. I didn't say I was your sister. It was fun, hearing them talk about you. But then they began to say you had a lover.

A pause.

ABELARD. No, there is no way they can know about Heloise.

DENISE. They said she is thirteen.

ABELARD. Well, there you are. She's seventeen. Convents are like… great forests, full of squawks and noises and nonsense.

DENISE. They said she is the niece of a canon at Notre Dame.

A pause.

It's dangerous, Peter.

ABELARD. Dangerous? Not at all. I am a great success. Her uncle loves me. The King himself has asked me to preach to him. This is a new age, my sister! There is a liberty of thought here in Paris, we make new discoveries every day, the books of classical learning open their secrets to us, we are running, full tilt, towards a wonderful future. With the new philosophy we will understand creation. We will see the face of God, fully. Know Him fully. And I am a leader in all this, with nothing to fear.

DENISE. Oh, I hope not.

A pause.

Now, in this shining new city, is there a tavern low enough for a country girl to sit with her randy philosopher brother, and have a drink?

ABELARD. Oh, we have everything.

They exit.

Scene Five

The journey to BERNARD*'s monastery at Clairvaux.*

Music.

Enter a MONK *in Cistercian robes. He drops dead.*

Enter ALBERIC *and* LOTHOLF. LOTHOLF *limps.* ALBERIC *has twinges in his back and is in a filthy temper.*

LOTHOLF. My feet are bad.

They walk on in silence.

My feet are very bad.

They walk on in silence.

There's stuff growing between my toes.

ALBERIC. Will you be quiet about your feet! I do not want to hear about your feet! I am sick of your feet!

LOTHOLF. But the stuff between my toes, it's growing! It's like plants!

ALBERIC. If you say *one more word* about your feet, I'll kill you. Right? I will kill.

They walk on in silence.

LOTHOLF. Why do we have to walk, anyway?

ALBERIC. Bernard is famous for the simple life. A lot of self-denial.

LOTHOLF. Oh, horrible.

ALBERIC. A lot of fasting, a lot of doing without. It's all about coming to know yourself.

LOTHOLF. I know my feet.

ALBERIC *just controls himself.*

ALBERIC. To ride up to his monastery with horse and carriage would not create a good impression. If we want him to help us, we must show we can mortify the flesh.

LOTHOLF. I've mortified my feet.

ALBERIC *loses all self-control and throws himself with a cry onto the ground, hitting it with his fists and feet.* LOTHOLF *sees the dead* MONK.

Alberic.

ALBERIC (*pointing up at him*). Prepare for death.

LOTHOLF. No, Alberic, look.

ALBERIC *looks. He stands.*

A pause.

ALBERIC. He's in the robes of a Cistercian. He must be from the monastery.

LOTHOLF. Fast asleep. Not such a hard life. (*Approaches the* MONK.) Brother? Can you help us on our way?

He stops. He looks beneath the cowl. The MONK *is dead.*

He's got pus in his mouth!

LOTHOLF *swings away and retches.* ALBERIC *backs away.*
And now two MONKS *come on, moving slowly. They carry a*
crude stretcher. They see the dead MONK, *run to him and put*
him onto the stretcher. They are carrying him away.

ALBERIC (*calling out to them*). Is there sickness at the
monastery?

The two MONKS *stop dead still, staring at* ALBERIC.

A pause.

1ST MONK. No. Only starvation.

LOTHOLF. Oh, that's all right then.

1ST MONK. There's plenty of prayer.

The two MONKS *exit, running with their load.*

LOTHOLF. Can you eat prayers? I can't. I can't bite on endless
amens.

ALBERIC. This is life and death. Way beyond food.

Enter a MAD MONK. *There is blood down one side of his*
robe. His hands are hidden.

MAD MONK. Have you got the sign?

ALBERIC. What sign, brother?

MAD MONK. Of the nail of the cross. I have. Do you want to
see it?

The MAD MONK *shows his hand. It is mutilated and covered*
in blood. LOTHOLF *is revolted.* ALBERIC *is fascinated.*

LOTHOLF. He's hammered a nail into his hand!

MAD MONK. I'm going to show Jesus. Won't he be pleased.

He exits, on his erratic line. ALBERIC *and* LOTHOLF *look*
at each other, dumbfounded. A MONK WITH A WHIP,
stripped to the waist, enters running.

MONK WITH WHIP. Morti me offerens!

He whips himself, screams and nearly falls.

Morti me offerens!

He whips himself, screams and nearly falls.

Morti me offerens!

He whips himself, screams and nearly falls. He exits.
ALBERIC *and* LOTHOLF *look around, wondering who will appear next.*

LOTHOLF. I have a very bad feeling.

ALBERIC. I find it strangely attractive.

BERNARD *enters, walking calmly. He stops and waits, absolutely still.* ALBERIC *and* LOTHOLF *stare at him, mesmerised.*

A pause.

BERNARD (*to* LOTHOLF). Your feet are bad.

LOTHOLF. Terrible.

BERNARD. Let me see.

BERNARD *kneels on one knee, waiting.* LOTHOLF *hesitates, then sits down and pulls off his rag-bound shoes.*

LOTHOLF. When your feet go, I mean what are you? You're not human any more.

He reveals his foot. It is filthy and covered in blisters and blood. BERNARD *takes the foot in both hands, almost with reverence, and looks at it.*

ALBERIC. Brother, we are looking for Abbot Bernard. Is he at the monastery?

BERNARD. I am Bernard.

Very slowly and very deliberately, and to the amazement of ALBERIC *and* LOTHOLF, BERNARD *lowers his head and begins to clean* LOTHOLF's *filthy foot with long licks of his tongue.*

LOTHOLF. Please, please. Oh dear oh dear.

BERNARD *lifts* LOTHOLF *onto his shoulder and is carrying him off.*

ALBERIC (*following*). A saint! A saint! He's a saint!

They exit.

Scene Six

In the monastery of Clairvaux.

Enter ALBERIC *and* LOTHOLF.

LOTHOLF. It's three o'clock in the morning, and we've sung matins already. And we had to sleep in boxes, wooden boxes! And where are all the monks? There were only fifteen at matins. And they could hardly speak, let alone sing. And as for *him*, he wasn't there at all.

ALBERIC. Don't you hear it?

LOTHOLF. Hear what?

ALBERIC. It's like a note. A constant harmony. It's passing through the air, through the walls, through you and me.

LOTHOLF (*listens, then shakes his head*). Nothing.

ALBERIC. I think it's the singing of angels.

LOTHOLF. We've not eaten anything for hours, that's all. It's getting to your ears.

BERNARD *enters, with a* MONK *who is carrying a tray. On the tray there is a jug and two small pieces of bread.*

BERNARD. You were at matins?

ALBERIC. Yes.

LOTHOLF. Yes.

BERNARD. I spent the night in the woods. Have you had breakfast?

LOTHOLF. No!

ALBERIC. No, brother.

BERNARD. Then please do.

The MONK *offers the tray. They stare at the pieces of bread. They lift them. The* MONK *pours a little warm water upon each piece.*

A little warm water on your bread? It is a luxury I, myself, usually avoid. I rarely drink water, warm or of any kind. But guests are very welcome to it.

ALBERIC *and* LOTHOLF *fall upon the bread and stuff it into their mouths. They look for crumbs upon the floor, find a few and eat them.* BERNARD *waits calmly until they have finished. He nods to the* MONK, *who exits.*

I was in the woods, praying for your mentor, William. The news you brought of him troubled me. I love that man, he was mother to my soul. He saw my calling before I did, and encouraged me to become a monk. He is a great man, even though he is a scholar. (*Smiles.*) And now he sends me two of his little ones. I am moved.

A pause.

This Peter Abelard...

LOTHOLF. It is because of him William fell ill. He sucked the life out of him, with his hellish arguments, like he was a devil.

BERNARD. I doubt that Abelard is a devil. He is a soul which has lost its way on its journey. He is in error. Error can be corrected.

ALBERIC. But how? He carries everything before him. The young flock to his school. The King has given him his favour.

BERNARD (*strangely*). Ah, the mighty King of France.

ALBERIC. And Abelard is brilliant. When you argue with him, it's as if you've fallen in a mill race. Nothing you can think of, nothing you can say, stops you rushing towards the wheel. And it crushes you.

LOTHOLF. Hits you on the head...

ALBERIC. And you come out the other side mangled and broken, with his students looking down on you, laughing. There *must* be arguments against his heathen logic. Help us, Magister.

BERNARD (*sharply*). Don't call me that! I am not a teacher. There is nothing to teach. All that we need, God reveals to us.

LOTHOLF. But you're starving –

BERNARD. True wisdom is given, it cannot be learnt! If you wish to be wise, little ones, leave the cloister schools of

Paris, the clever-clever arguments and disputations of 'Magister this' and 'Magister that'. Go to nature, alone, go to the raw creation of the Almighty. You will find something far greater in the woods, in stones, in trees, than you ever will in books.

ALBERIC. Forgive me, Abbot Bernard, but Abelard would laugh at that. And all his creatures along with him.

BERNARD. Why do you hate him so? Does he hurt your pride?

ALBERIC. No, I've not come here for myself.

BERNARD. My son, you are wreathed in the rags of self-regard. You envy Abelard's success, you wish the fashionable world knelt before you, not him.

ALBERIC. Abbot, you – cut a window to my soul.

BERNARD. Beware the desire for increase in merit.

ALBERIC. But you don't realise the power of this new logic! We must prepare against it. We must develop counter-arguments. We must study, we must arm ourselves.

BERNARD (*touching* ALBERIC'*s face*). No no no no no, my dear. Sufficient unto the day is the evil thereof.

A pause.

I came to this valley in this forest, two years ago. There were thirty of us. We found this building, deserted. Wooden, rough. We slept in the lofts. We had wooden boxes for beds. Some of my companions have left, some have died. I myself have been ill for the past year. I set a strict rule, you see. The rule to the dot, to the letter, of the instruction given us by the blessed St Benedict, telling us what the life of a monk should be! The silence. The endless prayer. The endless work. The denial of more than feelings, the denial of the senses themselves, I am talking of… peace. Perfect peace.

ALBERIC. Yes.

BERNARD. And if it is the will of God that this Abbey prosper, then the rule will hold. Others will come, as you have.

LOTHOLF (*panicking*). We're not staying, are we, Alberic…

ALBERIC *does not hear him.*

BERNARD (*iron in his voice*). We will gain strength. We will
have the power of the early fathers, the first monks, who
went to the desert and lived upon nothing but the bread and
the water of their mighty faith. And this place will be an
instrument for the purpose of God. From Clairvaux a new
purpose will shine, from it paths of the spirit will radiate out
through all of France, through this vile, evil, demon-ridden
world of barbarism and heresy and kings in fine clothes
eating fine meats and heretic scholars in cathedral cloisters.

He stops, overcome, fighting for breath. He retches.
ALBERIC *goes to help him.* BERNARD *waves him away,
with a violent gesture. He composes himself. He smiles.*

So though we are few, and sick, we are still here. Waiting for
God's strength. Like the lilies in the field, we grow. We *are.*

A silence.

ALBERIC. But... but what shall we do about Abelard?

BERNARD. Nothing. Wait. Watch. His sin is pride in his
intellect. He will overreach himself, the proud always do.
When you have rested, go back to Paris. My little ones, my
children... be the eyes and ears of Clairvaux.

*He kisses one then the other. He walks away, but then turns
back.*

If you wish to stay for the day and work in the fields, they
are sadly neglected. Pull up weeds. (*Smiles.*) Each one a little
Aristotle, to be uprooted.

BERNARD *exits, exhausted by talking to them.*

LOTHOLF. He's a madman. He's half-dead. Why did William
send us here? Bernard's got no influence, no power.

ALBERIC. Oh yes he has.

Scene Seven

The court of Louis VI.

ABELARD *is preaching to* KING LOUIS. *There are* STUDENTS *of* ABELARD, COURTIERS, *and* HELOISE *and* FULBERT *are there. During the scene, the* COURTIERS *at times whisper amongst themselves, spreading the instant myths of the court.*

ABELARD. All excellence comes from the knowledge of God's nature. We therefore take up the sword of human reasoning, to know God more. I am of the opinion that no scientific reasoning is improper for any religious person. The Almighty is known as 'The Spirit of Knowledge' – Isaiah, eleventh chapter, second verse. God is pleased that we reason. How far, then, should we take seriously, those who deny that knowledge can lead us to know the Spirit of Knowledge? Not at all. If God needed madmen to know and interpret his will, would he not have created us all insane at birth?

There is amusement amongst the COURTIERS *at this.*

God has given us the ability to think, to reason, to deduce. Why? Because He wants us to understand His creation, to understand ourselves, to progress to a full knowledge of the world so we can know Him fully. He has set us on a path from ignorance to knowledge. He wants us to be awake in the world! For example, it is contemptible to say a prayer that you do not understand. People who don't know Latin, let them pray in French!

A flicker of unease amongst the court.

For isn't it our nature to want to know? And our nature comes from God's nature: our minds, though fallen and imperfect, are in his image. It seems to me to be ridiculous to assert that when the prophets wrote about the Holy Trinity, they were like brute beasts and did not understand their own words! God gave us reason, and language, and in language logic, so that we may come to know Him. In the name of the Father, the Son and the Holy Ghost, for ever and ever, Amen.

ALL. Amen.

LOUIS. Pretty, very pretty. More religion in it than I thought there'd be.

Giggles in the court.

ABELARD. You did ask me to preach a sermon, Your Majesty.

LOUIS. Mm. And what do you think, Canon Fulbert? Of your protégé's effort?

FULBERT. It is very modern, Your Majesty.

LOUIS. Is that a good thing?

FULBERT. Oh, excellent.

LOUIS. I liked the bit about madmen. Who can you mean, Abelard? Not that monk in a wooden box, out in the woods?

ABELARD. I meant no one in particular, Your Majesty.

LOUIS. Testicles, testicles, Abelard.

Delight amongst the COURTIERS *at this.*

COURTIERS. Testicles, testicles – His Majesty said testicles – he said testicles to Abelard!

LOUIS. What I enjoy about this fashion for theology, is the way you teachers, and preachers, and monks are always *cutting* each other to the very death with your arguments. Theology in Paris these days is more entertaining than wrestling matches or dancing bears!

COURTIERS. Monks and bears – monks and bears – His Majesty compares monks to bears!

LOUIS. But tell me, dear Magister Peter, wasn't Aristotle, from whom all this praise of science comes, a heathen? Well, he was born before Christ, so he must have been a heathen, mustn't he? That's logical. (*To the* COURTIERS.) Goodness! I do believe I have gone dialectical.

COURTIERS. Dia-what? – 'Lectical! – His Majesty has gone dialectical! –

LONE VOICE. What's dialectical?

COURTIERS. Sh!

ABELARD. Your Majesty's intelligence shines upon us all.

LOUIS. Don't overdo the courtier, Peter.

A sharp breath from a COURTIER.

ABELARD. Forgive me, Your Majesty.

LOUIS. So. How could a pagan like Aristotle, soaked in the belief of false gods, hold any truth for a Christian? Eh? (*To the* COURTIERS.) A pretty point, eh? Eh?

COURTIERS. Very pretty, Your Majesty – radiant – a flower of a philosophical point, Your Majesty –

And they burst into applause.

All turn to ABELARD, *who is looking at* HELOISE. *An understanding passes between them – they both know the argument.*

ABELARD. When God created the world, did men see what He had done?

LOUIS (*a brief pause*). Yes.

ABELARD. So God has made Himself manifest from the moment of creation, in the world. Which pagans saw, as much as we Christians do?

LOUIS. Yes yes.

ABELARD. So does it not follow that the pagans could gain knowledge of God from the natural world? And reason is part of the natural world, so they could use it, to know God, even before He had revealed himself in Christ. I believe that even Plato knew in his heart of the Son, the Father and the Holy Ghost, the Trinity itself.

A silence.

LOUIS. Beautiful, beautiful. An argument like a cloth of gold, Abelard, laid out before us.

He claps his hands. The COURTIERS *follow, but stop at once when* LOUIS *begins to speak again.*

But if the pagans, the Platos and the Aristotles were so wise, one wonders why God sent His son down to us at all. He could have thrown down books in Greek.

Sharp breaths from the COURTIERS.

I heard that said the other day, actually, about your talk of
revelation in pagan writings. Said by a bishop.

A silence. The COURTIERS *wait.*

ABELARD. A stupid bishop.

LOUIS. Can there be such a thing?

ABELARD. There are many wonders in this world.

A moment, LOUIS *looking disapproving. Then he smiles and
laughs, applauding. All applaud. With a wave of his hand,*
LOUIS *signals that the discussion is over. Dancing amongst
the* COURTIERS *begins.* LOUIS *gestures to* FULBERT *and*
HELOISE. *They approach.*

LOUIS. And this is?

FULBERT (*very pleased*). My niece Heloise, Your Majesty.

LOUIS. The young woman whom, I understand, Magister
Abelard here teaches?

FULBERT. Indeed, Your Majesty.

LOUIS. That makes her something of a treasure in our city.

FULBERT. I took her into my house. She is the child of my
elder sister, who was an Abbess in the south, near Perigueux.
Her convent was stormed by heretics. But she took up with
the leader of that godless band, and had this innocent child.

LOUIS. A heretic Abbess for a mother. I hope you teach her
well, Abelard.

ABELARD. I try to, Your Majesty.

LOUIS *does know the rumour. He looks at* HELOISE *with a
smile. She shifts, uncomfortably.*

LOUIS. And strictly.

ABELARD. Oh, I am strict with her, Your Majesty.

LOUIS. I expect you are. (*A brief pause.*) Please enjoy yourself,
my dear. Perhaps dance with your teacher?

HELOISE. Thank you, Your Majesty.

ABELARD. Your Majesty.

ABELARD *and* HELOISE *join the dance. After a while, a* CHAMBERLAIN *makes his way to* LOUIS. *He says something into* LOUIS*'s ear, who laughs.*

LOUIS. Really? Let him in.

CHAMBERLAIN. Your Majesty, there is a sanitary problem.

LOUIS. What are you talking about?

CHAMBERLAIN. Your Majesty, the smell –

LOUIS (*snaps*). I said let him in!

He claps his hands. The dancing stops.

Abelard, Abelard! Something of interest for you here, out of a wooden box!

COURTIERS. Box? Present in a box? – Oh good! A surprise – surprise, a surprise – the King has a surprise...

The CHAMBERLAIN *goes out. He comes back in.* BERNARD *enters. The* COURTIERS *back away at the smell.*

COURTIERS. He stinks – rotten flesh – bad cheese...

CHAMBERLAIN. Brother Bernard, Abbot of the Cistercian monastery of Clairvaux, Your Majesty, with a petition.

LOUIS. Brother Abbot, we are having something of a little party of sermons here. Please do join us.

BERNARD *vomits copiously down his robe. He almost falls. He steadies himself. The court is transfixed.* ABELARD *smiles.*

BERNARD. Louis. The King of Heaven and Earth has given you a kingdom in this world and he will give you one in that which is to come. Why, then, do you persecute His Archbishop of Sens?

A shocked silence.

Why have you stolen his lands? Why have you uprooted his vineyards? Fined his friends and relations? Driven his peasants from their farms? Why did you lift your hand against Christ's wife, Holy Church herself? I come as a simple monk, to say restore the Archbishop's lands. Make your peace with him. Be just. If you do not... (*Points at* LOUIS.) Who dares abuse Christ's bride? Who dares to besmirch her? Torment her? Tear her wedding dress? Who dares not to fear the wrath of her husband, our Lord Jesus Christ?

A silence.

Amen!

The shock continues for a moment, then FULBERT *falls to his knees.* COURTIERS *follow.*

FULBERT. Amen!

COURTIERS. Amen! Amen! Amen!...

    ABELARD *and* HELOISE *have not knelt.*

LOUIS. Abelard? What do you make of this?

    BERNARD *turns to* ABELARD. *They stare at each other. The court is tense.*

ABELARD. The Brother Abbot's cause is just.

LOUIS. You agree with him?

ABELARD. Render unto Caesar what is Caesar's, unto God what is God's.

LOUIS. Oh yes, specially when land is involved. Render that to God!

    He stands, in a fury.

You men of the church stick together. Logicians or vomiters, theologians, monks, bishops. You're all the same in the end. The Archbishop will get his wretched farms back. Sermons, dancing, done for today.

    He storms off. The COURTIERS *run after him.*

FULBERT. Thank you, Peter. My little girl met His Majesty, and because of you!

ABELARD (*looking at* BERNARD, *who looks back*). Yes, Canon.

FULBERT. Come, my dear.

    HELOISE *wants to say something to* ABELARD, *who shakes his head.* HELOISE *and* FULBERT *exit.* ABELARD *and* BERNARD *are alone.*

Scene Eight

BERNARD *and* ABELARD *alone*.

BERNARD. I admonish you.

ABELARD. You do what?

BERNARD. Our meeting is not by accident. It is by the hand of Christ, so that I may admonish you.

A pause. Then ABELARD *laughs*.

ABELARD. Don't be ridiculous.

BERNARD. Turn away from error, Peter Abelard.

ABELARD. You are a ridiculous man.

BERNARD. Abandon your teachings. Cease to pervert the minds of the young.

ABELARD. I liked the vomiting. What did you do, rush in with a cup of vegetable soup in your mouth? A good trick, Abbot. But for ignorant peasants at country fairs, not for a man of His Majesty's intelligence.

A silence. BERNARD *looks at* ABELARD, *unmoved*.

BERNARD. Your doctrine on the Holy Trinity is heretical.

ABELARD. Really? Oh dear me.

BERNARD. The Trinity is one. Mystically one. Indivisible. You teach that Father, Son and Holy Ghost are individual. (*Becomes angry*.) All your teaching is riddled with 'the individual'. The single human spirit, equal to the Holy Spirit. Your theology is all 'I', 'I', it is all of the self. It is vanity and conceit, it puts man before God.

ABELARD. You are well informed about my seminars, Abbot.

BERNARD. I have eyes and ears.

ABELARD. I don't doubt your spies are everywhere. All reporting back to Clairvaux. (*A pause*.) But we're alone here, for a moment. Just two men, standing on the surface of God's creation. So let's be honest with each other. I mean, you are a fake, aren't you? Everything I've heard of your abbey, full of starving young men, the deprived, the half-witted and the unhappy from all over France, witnessing angels and visions in the fields... it must be fakery. What do you do, put mould in the bread? Or is it just the power of your person? Actually, the light does shine out of your eyes. You look the part of a saint, perfectly. But you are a charlatan. Admit it, just between the two of us.

BERNARD. There is a third in this room. Listening to all we say.

ABELARD. You don't really believe that.

BERNARD *smiles*.

You really believe you see our Lord?

BERNARD. Yes. Don't you?

ABELARD. He talks to you?

BERNARD. He has always talked to His prophets.

ABELARD. Of whom you are one?

BERNARD *is silent*.

And you accuse me of conceit? What does He look like?

BERNARD. Be careful, Peter Abelard.

ABELARD. No! This vision, this personal appearance, granted to you but to so few others... how tall is it? Is it bearded? Is it robed? Has it dragged the cross itself, up the steps of the King's palace to be with us? Does it look suspiciously French, or is it Jewish, for our Lord was a Semite you know, perhaps with a dark skin, rather like a Saracen. I suspect that the real Christ, if you met him, would be something of a shock. So! Where is He then exactly, in this room?

BERNARD. Behind you.

A pause.

Turn and look at Him.

A pause.

Have faith. Look at your Saviour.

ABELARD *does not*.

ABELARD. You are more dangerous than I thought. You believe in what you say.

BERNARD. *You* are more dangerous than *I* thought. You believe in nothing.

ABELARD. That is a slander. If I acknowledge your sincerity, why can't you acknowledge mine?

BERNARD. Because, in my hearing, you have mocked Christ himself.

ABELARD. I have only mocked your delusion.

BERNARD. No, you cannot see your error. It is your teaching that leads you to mock faith in our Lord.

ABELARD. My teaching tries to *understand* faith, to make our belief strong.

BERNARD. It will only weaken belief. I hear that you begin to question the miracles of our Lord. You doubt whether He fed the five thousand, raised Lazarus from the dead, walked upon the waters of Galilee.

ABELARD. The parables have hidden meaning.

BERNARD. You teach that they did not happen.

ABELARD. I teach their meaning, which is beyond the trivial matter of whether five fish actually became five thousand, or water turned into wine.

BERNARD. Can't you see the road that you are on? Error after error, stretching into a future in which all religion will be destroyed by your vanity, your doubt, your conceit of human reason and its infernal child, logic.

ABELARD. I must seek faith with the mind God gave me.

BERNARD. I warn you, with all the authority I have as a priest of Christ's church. You may not think and dispute on faith as you please. You may not wander here and there, through the wastes of opinion, the byways of error. God encloses us with boundaries. We are restrained within unchanging limits. Faith is not a matter of opinion. It is a certainty.

ABELARD. Dispute with me in public.

BERNARD. Never.

ABELARD. Argue. In true and honest debate. Let our hearers judge.

BERNARD. There is nothing to argue, nothing to judge. I will not go down into the bear pit of pagan logic, to be cut to pieces by your tricks of speech, Peter Abelard. You are the charlatan, not I.

ABELARD. This must be resolved between us.

BERNARD. It is resolved.

A pause. Then ABELARD *turns away, angrily. He stops when* BERNARD *speaks.*

Stay upon this path and you will ruin yourself. I beg you, correct your errors, my little one. Come to me.

ABELARD *turns on him, with contempt.*

ABELARD. Who do you think you are? My mother?

ABELARD *exits.* BERNARD *pauses, then turns, looking at someone.*

Scene Nine

A narrow alley, round the back of Notre Dame. ALBERIC, LOTHOLF *and a* YOUNG WOMAN – *a prostitute who is with* LOTHOLF – *are hanging about in the alley, looking one way then the other.*

LOTHOLF. He does walk down here?

ALBERIC. Yes yes, this way round the back of Notre Dame, at noon every day. It's his daily devotional.

WOMAN. Is this church stuff? I don't want anything to do with it, if it's church stuff.

LOTHOLF. You know what this is about, it's about what you saw, so shut up.

WOMAN. Pay me. Half now.

LOTHOLF *looks at* ALBERIC, *who looks fed up.*
Reluctantly he gives the WOMAN *some money. They look up and down the alley.*

LOTHOLF. There he is! I want to give it to him. This is all thanks to me, you know.

ALBERIC. Just make him squirm.

FULBERT *enters. He is reading a small book.*

LOTHOLF. Canon Fulbert!

FULBERT *is startled. At once he fumbles in his clothing and pulls out a small knife.*

ALBERIC. We're not thieves, Canon.

FULBERT. Who are you then?

LOTHOLF. We are students of the late William of Champeaux, who is now with the angels.

FULBERT. May his soul rest in peace.

ALBERIC. Amen.

LOTHOLF. Amen.

ALBERIC *and* LOTHOLF *look at the* WOMAN.

WOMAN. Amen. (*Laughs.*) Ha!

FULBERT (*knife still out*). I am surprised to see men who were of William's school, in the company of a painted thing from Babylon.

WOMAN. Thank you very much.

ALBERIC. Sadly, my companion is weak in the flesh. We visited the Abbey of Clairvaux and the self-denial there so shocked him, ever since he has swung the other way.

LOTHOLF. I can't get enough of everything.

FULBERT. I could imagine that a stay at Clairvaux could fill the mind with craving for rich meats. But what is this to do with me?

ALBERIC. Tell the good Canon.

LOTHOLF. Well, I was with Franny here, out in the fields. Well, first we did it in a ditch.

WOMAN. Side of a ditch.

FULBERT *stares at them*.

LOTHOLF. Yeah in a sort of hollow.

WOMAN. Me on top. So I could keep a lookout, for people in the fields.

LOTHOLF. I wanted to go doggy fashion. Said I'd keep a lookout.

WOMAN. I didn't trust him. (*To the* CANON.) Would you? There's always people in the fields. Doing it in the open air has big problems.

FULBERT. I don't know who you are, or what you want, but I am not standing here to listen to this, for one more breath in my body...

ALBERIC. You have to! Don't you understand, you stupid, vain, foolish man, don't you know your life is about to change utterly? (*To* LOTHOLF *and the* WOMAN.) Do it to him!

LOTHOLF. I was really hot for her again. We went in the wood.

WOMAN. Horrible wood.

LOTHOLF. We thought 'lie down under the trees'. But it was too thick.

WOMAN. Mossy bank? Forget it.

LOTHOLF. The peasants cut the trees, so they branch out, from the bole of the trunks. It gives them more firewood. They do that on my father's farm...

ALBERIC. Do it!

LOTHOLF. There was this sound.

WOMAN. A girl breathing. You know. Coming.

FULBERT. I...

LOTHOLF. And we saw them. Cos of the way the trees are cut, you can make a kind of nest. That's what they'd done.

WOMAN. A cosy nest up in a tree. Like a strange bird. But not with feathers, cos they were nude.

LOTHOLF. Yeah, nude.

WOMAN. Legs, dangling in the branches.

LOTHOLF. Bits of clothes on twigs.

WOMAN. Fucking, face to face.

ALBERIC. It was your niece and Peter Abelard!

LOTHOLF (*furious*). You bastard! You bastard! I'm telling!

   FULBERT *is dead still. A long silence.*

ALBERIC. Canon?

FULBERT. Why do you come up to me and tell me these lies, this filth?

LOTHOLF. Not lies at all.

ALBERIC. It is filth, though.

FULBERT. You're demons. Demons lie and deceive. You've come out of the earth to tell vile, terrible lies about my lovely little girl! I abjure you, go back down to hell.

ALBERIC. Canon, the rumours about them are everywhere. The whole town knows about Abelard and your 'lovely girl'. Women in taverns, baker's boys, ostlers, peasants in the fields, nuns in the convents, even the King knows.

FULBERT. Demons even lie about lies…

LOTHOLF. We've got proof.

WOMAN. A bit of nest.

   She laughs. LOTHOLF *takes out a piece of cloth, torn from* HELOISE*'s dress. There is a leaf stuck to it. He gives it to* FULBERT, *who stares at it, dumbly, then pulls the leaf away and looks at it.*

ALBERIC. Look for them yourself. You'll find them. Where are they now?

FULBERT. He is giving her her daily instruction, in my home, in the room above the… (*Pauses.*) Garden. (*Pauses.*) I must go home. I must go.

   He stumbles away and exits. ALBERIC *and* LOTHOLF *jump up and down with joy.*

LOTHOLF. Let's get drunk. And eat... tête de veau! The head of a calf, boiled in white wine, washed down with lashings of burgundy.

ALBERIC (*savouring the moment*). Isn't... isn't... telling the Canon of Abelard, tastier than anything you could stuff or swill down you?

WOMAN. Other half please.

LOTHOLF. I don't think we've done with you yet.

WOMAN. If it's the two of you it's double.

LOTHOLF. Let's go!

They swing the WOMAN *between them and rush off with her, the three of them laughing.*

Scene Ten

FULBERT*'s house.*

FULBERT *is pounding a door with his fists. He looks at his hands. They are bloody.*

FULBERT. Abelard, Abelard, you must be in there. Open this door.

He pauses to recover his breath.

That is a command from the master of this house!

Nothing happens. He breathes. Then he looks up. He rushes away and exits.

A moment, the stage empty.

He re-enters, rushing. It is as if he is in the room above. He lies down, trying to see through a crack in the floorboards.

You're in a room in my house, Abelard! How dare you not let me in to a room in my own house!

He pummels the floorboards with his fists. He sits up, nursing his hands.

Abelard! What are you doing to my little girl? I beg you.

He hears something. He stands and exits, rushing.

A moment's pause, the stage empty.

He re-enters. Mime: he bangs once upon the door. To his surprise it swings open. ABELARD *and* HELOISE *are revealed. They are standing formally, clothed. Each has a small book open. They look at* FULBERT *with vague smiles fixed upon their faces.*

A pause.

Why didn't you open the door at once?

A moment, all of them still.

HELOISE. Sorry, Uncle, have you been trying to get in?

FULBERT. Of course I've been trying to get in! I have all but broken my hands, trying to get in.

HELOISE. We were so intent on Juvenal's satire, that we did not hear you. Did we, Magister Abelard?

ABELARD. Indeed not. The senses die, when you read an eternal poet.

FULBERT. But suddenly the door was open!

A moment's hesitation.

HELOISE. Damp.

ABELARD. Yes. Your magnificent house is damp. The wood is young. It swells a little.

HELOISE. We have noticed it with the door.

ABELARD. Yes, swelling.

FULBERT. But the house is not that young!

ABELARD. But the wood is.

FULBERT (*hesitates*). Yes, the wood could be young.

ABELARD. Full of sap.

FULBERT. *What?*

A pause. ABELARD *and* HELOISE *have kept their pose.* FULBERT*'s anger is draining away.*

You are reading Juvenal.

HELOISE. Yes. *The Vanity of Human Wishes.*

FULBERT. Oh, my dear little one, I have been mistaken, haven't I?

HELOISE. In what, Uncle?

FULBERT. In this.

He takes out the piece of cloth given him by LOTHOLF. *It is the same as she is wearing in this scene.* ABELARD *and* HELOISE *stare at it.*

HELOISE. That is very like my dress. What does it mean?

FULBERT. It was given to me by... creatures, who stopped me by our church. They said it was from a wood.

HELOISE. Wood?

FULBERT (*shamefaced*). Heloise, can I look at your dress?

HELOISE. Of course, Uncle. Do you want me to withdraw and take it off?

A silence.

He breaks down. She has, for the moment, outfaced him.

FULBERT. I have had such a shock. It made me forget how vicious the world can be toward the pure. How the innocent are besmirched, by the envy and hatred of demons. (*Going to them.*) Forgive me, I am so sorry.

He attempts to embrace HELOISE. *She recoils. The posed picture that the lovers have been presenting is broken.* FULBERT *sees that* HELOISE*'s dress is open down the back, revealing the length of her side. She backs away holding the dress around her.* ABELARD *is straightening his own clothing, having also dressed hurriedly.* FULBERT *advances on him, as to strike him.*

You low, you vile, you fiend of low, vile manhood, have you ruined what I love most in the world?

HELOISE. Uncle, no…

FULBERT (*turns on her*). Not one word to me! Do you want to be whipped and drowned in a pond, like a village harlot, is that what my girl wants? (*Turns back to* ABELARD.) How long?

ABELARD. Since we first met in this room.

HELOISE. From the first moment.

FULBERT. How often?

HELOISE. Whenever we could.

FULBERT. I told you not to speak. I want to believe that you are an innocent in this, that it is this man who has led you astray, and so greatly abused his position of a teacher of religion.

ABELARD. That is true, Canon. I am to blame. I have preyed upon her.

FULBERT. Bird of prey! On my girl!

HELOISE (*to* ABELARD). No, I have preyed upon you, as much as you have preyed upon me!

ABELARD. It is my corruption that has led to this.

HELOISE. There is nothing corrupt about us!

ABELARD. Canon, believe me, the blame is mine.

HELOISE. Blame? What is blame to do with us? (*Turns to* FULBERT.) We are man and woman, equal in love.

FULBERT *begins to weep. He points at her dress.*

FULBERT. That is a patch in that dress, isn't it? Finely done, but a patch.

HELOISE. Oh, Uncle dearest, can you find it in your heart to be glad for me?

FULBERT. Glad? (*Collects himself. Fury washes into him.*) Glad!? That you have turned from your journey to Christ and his city, and have taken a road deep in filth, that leads to Babylon? Glad that you and your fork-tongued teacher have dishonoured my family? Made me a laughing stock! Baker's boys, even the King, they said, know of your doings! In my house, in trees!

ABELARD. Your family's honour will be safe.

FULBERT. Safe? My honour?

ABELARD. I will ask you for her hand.

FULBERT. To do what with it?

ABELARD. To marry her.

HELOISE *starts*.

I'll marry her.

FULBERT. Oh, will you!

ABELARD. I will marry her at once.

FULBERT (*struggling with himself before speaking*). Oh, Peter! (*Pauses.*) Peter Abelard, you were my protégé. I had ambitions for you. Twenty, thirty years from now, who knows, the throne of Peter itself… But because you have put your hands upon my little girl, you will be a wretched, lowly married cleric. But yes, yes. Right the wrong you have done my family. Marry her.

HELOISE. But *I* won't marry *him*.

They stare at her.

FULBERT. That is not for the woman to say.

HELOISE (*to* ABELARD). I won't marry you. I don't want to be the woman running your household, I don't want children pulling at my skirts, at my body, I don't want to be the ageing, bitter crone, standing at the back of the church, loathed by my husband. I will be your lover, only. I will live with you in Babylon. I will be your mistress, your whore, but not your wife.

She goes to ABELARD *and embraces him.* FULBERT *raises his fists in a rage.*

Scene Eleven

Two years later.

Brittany coast. Clifftop.

HELOISE *and* DENISE, *wrapped up against the wind.*

HELOISE. Is that your father in that boat?

DENISE. Yes. He's setting the crab pots.

HELOISE. I didn't know he did that.

DENISE. You've not noticed he likes to think he's a fisherman, even though he's a farmer?

HELOISE *does not reply.*

He has always wanted to be what he is not. It's a family trait.

HELOISE. Meaning?

DENISE *does not reply.*

DENISE. My mother used to bring me up here, on the cliffs, to watch him taking the crab boat out.

HELOISE. Meaning?

DENISE *does not reply.*

Meaning, why don't I hold my son up to watch his grandfather put pots out for crabs? As you were held up, as Peter was?

DENISE. No.

HELOISE. Start him young, to love his family?

DENISE. It's not for me to say.

HELOISE. But you do say. You think I neglect my baby.

DENISE. This is a farm. People work hard. They don't have time to bring up...

She stops.

HELOISE. Bring up the bastard of a Parisian slut, dumped on them by the absent first son? And a very strange, uncountrified kind of slut, who lies around the house reading books all day.

DENISE. I didn't mean…

HELOISE. Yes you did.

A pause. She looks out to sea.

You make love, everywhere. Every way you can. Every day
something new happens. And even when the crisis comes,
and people are shouting at you, and you find you are pregnant,
and you're smuggled out of Paris dressed as a nun…

DENISE (*giggles*). He did disguise you as a nun, didn't he.

HELOISE. The whore of Babylon in holy clothes…

They laugh. HELOISE *is pleased.*

Oh, Denise, even when we were betrayed to my uncle and
every day was like the end of the world, I knew I was alive.
Then it stopped. And I found myself here. Grey sea and
boats, dull green land and sheep. And little Astralabe,
screaming every day. And nothing happening, for two years.

DENISE. Welcome to real life.

HELOISE. I want it all to start again.

DENISE. It is.

A long pause.

See that man, climbing over the wall down there?

A pause.

HELOISE. It's not Peter. He's limping. He's got no horse.

She recognises him. A pause.

Oh.

A pause.

Oh, is he hurt, what's happened?

She is about to rush off to greet him. DENISE *stops her.*

DENISE. No. Wait here. He can see us on the skyline, that's
why he's left the road. Wait for your lover with your back to
the sky, Heloise. You're older now. He hasn't seen you for
two years. You're beginning to change. Let him come up to
you slowly, to find out what you are.

They look at each other.

HELOISE. You've been kind, but I don't know if you love me.

DENISE. I love my brother.

HELOISE. But not his mistress.

DENISE. His love is my love.

HELOISE. I wish you understood. Peter and I aren't a family. We never will be.

DENISE (*with dislike*). What are you then?

HELOISE. We're warriors. Philosophical warriors. We're fighting in a war of ideas.

DENISE. And what is little Astralabe, a war orphan?

HELOISE (*facing her down*). Yes.

DENISE (*scoffs*). Fighting in a war.

HELOISE. Please understand. You're his sister. We must love each other.

DENISE *looks away in the direction of the approaching* ABELARD, *who is still offstage.*

DENISE. Have you seen my father's wound, from fighting with the King in Burgundy? No you haven't, have you. You don't do the daughterly things for the head of the household, like bathing his wound. (*A pause.*) It's never healed. It runs right from his waist to his armpit. In bad months, red lines run down to his groin, and it oozes and smells. But I fear wounds in your war of ideas could be worse. You could be forced to be an anchoress, walled up in a cave, being handed bread and water through a hole. Peter could be sent to a monastery with his tongue cut out, the great Peter Abelard, not able to speak another word until the end of his life. And they say they're burning heretics again, in the south. Have you thought of that? Thought what defeat could mean in your 'war of ideas'?

HELOISE. I must live this life with Peter.

DENISE. Oh yes, you must live your lives, the great scholars, the great lovers, the scandal and the wonder of the world, sung about in songs. But what about me? I'll bring up your child, I don't mind that. But… if Peter's come to take you back to Paris, I'll lie awake every night in terror for the both of you.

HELOISE. Oh, Denise, my dearest.

HELOISE *wants to go to comfort her, but* DENISE *turns away.* ABELARD *enters.*

ABELARD. I've been walking for a week. I was robbed, horse, money. (*Shrugs.*) But some Cluniac monks took pity on me. Brittany my Brittany, monks and bandits.

A pause. Then to HELOISE.

I saw you, against the sky.

HELOISE *runs to* ABELARD *and embraces him.*

HELOISE. So life is going to start again?

ABELARD. Yes! Yes!

They embrace. DENISE *turns away.*

End of Act One.

Interval.

ACT TWO

Scene One

FULBERT*'s house.*

HELOISE, ABELARD, FULBERT *and two of his* COUSINS. *They are heavy-looking, well-dressed men. They are all in an argument that has got out of control.*

ABELARD. I want to talk to her!

FULBERT. You said you would right the wrong you had done me. Instead you took her away to have your child...

1ST COUSIN. Bastard brat!

2ND COUSIN. Brat!

FULBERT. Now you bring her back, and put her in my house...

1ST COUSIN. Like it was a brothel!

2ND COUSIN. Brothel!

HELOISE. Uncle, Magister Abelard and I must talk...

FULBERT. Don't 'Magister' him with me, he's no teacher, no master...

1ST COUSIN. Dog off the street, with his cock up...

2ND COUSIN. Cock up!

1ST COUSIN. Mounting her like a common bitch!

2ND COUSIN. Common bitch!

HELOISE. Leave us alone!

ABELARD (*to the* 1ST COUSIN). Keep a civil tongue in your head. Or I will...

1ST COUSIN (*very threatening*). What? You will what, dog?

2ND COUSIN. Doggy doggy.

They all look at the 2ND COUSIN. *He gives an evil grin.*
His teeth are all black. Everyone is out of breath. They rest,
breathing heavily. Then FULBERT*'s anger swells again.*

FULBERT. How dare you treat me like this, bringing the thing I
have loved and you have wrecked with your… filthy, dirty,
practices… back to my house. And round you come…

1ST COUSIN. Sniffing.

FULBERT. Sniffing.

2ND COUSIN. Sniffing.

ABELARD. I want her to be in your house, with honour.

FULBERT. Then do something honourable.

ABELARD. You won't let her out of your sight! She and I
must speak.

A pause.

FULBERT (*close to* ABELARD). You are not going to further
insult this family. You are not going to carry on as you did
before.

1ST COUSIN (*goes close to* ABELARD *too*). No more
humping.

2ND COUSIN (*goes close too*). No more humping.

ABELARD. Thank you, gentlemen. All I beg is that you leave
us alone for a few minutes, so that we resolve this. Then all
of us can be at peace.

A pause.

FULBERT. The wood in the door is no longer young,
'Magister' Abelard.

FULBERT *and the two* COUSINS *exit*.

HELOISE. Get me out of this house.

ABELARD. Who were those men?

HELOISE. His cousins. Peter, I can't stay here.

ABELARD. My love, where else can you go?

HELOISE. Last night he came into my room. He stood at the foot of my bed. I pretended to be asleep, but half-opened my eyes. My uncle, a canon of the church... He was standing there staring down at me, with a candle in one hand and a knife in the other. And naked.

ABELARD. If he tries to do anything to you... I will kill...

HELOISE. Why kill? Just take me away. Put me in a room, above a tavern.

ABELARD. You know I can't do that.

HELOISE. Take me to your lodgings, then. Openly.

ABELARD. If we were married. Yes.

A pause.

HELOISE. Oh no.

ABELARD. We must find a way to marry.

HELOISE. No! Not after all we've said.

ABELARD. All you've said.

HELOISE. And which I say again. Give me love, not wedlock. Give me freedom, not chains.

ABELARD. I have always said that I would marry you.

HELOISE *turns away for a moment, collecting herself. Then she turns back at him.*

HELOISE. Remember what my uncle said, when he discovered us? If you marry me, you'll never be a candidate for the Vatican.

ABELARD. That's absurd.

HELOISE. Is it? Why? Isn't the Pope a man? And aren't you a better man than this Innocent the Second, whom Bernard is preaching as the true Pope. If Bernard of Clairvaux can have his candidate for Peter's Throne, why can't Heloise of Paris have hers?

ABELARD. This isn't worthy of you, it's just stupid.

HELOISE. Well, if you don't want to be Pope, do you want to be a cardinal?

ABELARD. Of course not.

HELOISE. An archbishop?

ABELARD. No.

HELOISE. A bishop.

ABELARD (*a slight hesitation*). No.

HELOISE. An abbot?

ABELARD *does not reply. A pause.*

You would be a wonderful abbot. Kind, impulsive but ever attentive, sending the brothers of your house into the world to spread learning and light. But you'll be no abbot, if you're married.

A pause.

ABELARD. Your uncle is the problem. I must put things in order.

HELOISE. Oh yes, put *me* in order. Put your lust in order.

ABELARD. Heloise, I've thought of something.

HELOISE. Oh, you've *thought* of something.

ABELARD. I have a plan.

HELOISE. Oh a plan! How masterful!

ABELARD. Marry me in secret.

She stares at him.

If you marry me in secret, your uncle's honour will be restored.

HELOISE. No, it's too late. We've driven him out of his mind.

ABELARD. No. He will see you as a respectably married woman. You will be able to live happily in his house. And I will visit, and sit at his table for dinner. And we will be at peace.

HELOISE. And are you going to end up as Pope, secretly married?

ABELARD. Yes. You'll live with me in the Vatican, disguised as a cardinal.

She relaxes and laughs.

HELOISE. Oh, Peter, I am so tired.

They hold each other.

ABELARD. This will work. This is excellent. A secret marriage.

HELOISE. When?

ABELARD. Now.

HELOISE. What?

ABELARD. I have a priest waiting.

HELOISE. Oh do you! So you came here with this arranged?

ABELARD. It is all thought out in every detail, it is perfect. The priest is waiting for us in the garden.

HELOISE. In the vegetable garden?

ABELARD. We will go down to him and he will marry us, tonight. This very moment.

HELOISE *is very distressed. She leans back in his arms, near to fainting.*

HELOISE. I wish to oppose you in this, but I cannot. I cannot oppose you in anything.

ABELARD. Do you agree, then? That this is our wedding?

HELOISE (*smiles*). Among the cabbages?

She steps back from him, holding his arms. She is very formal.

You are the sole possessor of my body and my will. God knows I seek nothing in you, but yourself. I simply want you. The name of wife may be sacred, but sweeter to me will always be the word 'mistress'.

ABELARD. My dear…

HELOISE. Be quiet. I am telling you that I will marry you.

She kneels before him.

Peter, against all my thoughts, my judgement, against the life I wish I could live, I will call you husband. (*Looks up.*) Now take me to the cabbages.

ABELARD (*taking her hand*). We climb out of the window.

HELOISE (*laughs*). Out of the window?

ABELARD. I've looked at it in daylight. It's simple…

She laughs again and they exit.

Scene Two

FULBERT*'s house. Garden, then room.*

Garden. The stage is empty for a moment. The 2ND COUSIN *appears. He urinates at the side of the garden, grunting.*

2ND COUSIN. Heloise Heloise, hunh hunh hunh, Heloise, hunh hunh.

Then a figure, in ecclesiastical dress, carrying a book and a crucifix, scuttles onto the stage. The 2ND COUSIN *sees him.*

Oi, what are you? Oi oi!

The FIGURE *starts, then exits, running. The* 2ND COUSIN *straightens his clothes, runs after him and exits.*

Room. FULBERT *and the* 1ST COUSIN *enter.* The 1ST COUSIN *has a whip on his belt. He carries a flagon of wine. Both have been drinking and are in an ugly mood.*

FULBERT. Abelard, are you in this room?

1ST COUSIN (*drinking a slug of wine*). The dogs have run off. The rabbits have scampered away, down their burrow. The breeding little pinky mice have…

FULBERT. No, they're in here! In a corner. Nude. They're very sly, very clever, they can do the deed anywhere. Sh, listen! (*A pause.*) They've dug a hole in the wall, they're doing it in the wall!

1ST COUSIN. They're not here, Fulbert.

FULBERT. We were watching the door all the time…

1ST COUSIN. Out of the window. Turned into crows by witchcraft. Flown off to a filthy nest.

FULBERT. He brought her back here, now he has stolen her again?

The 2ND COUSIN *enters, excited.*

2ND COUSIN. Priest.

1ST COUSIN. What priest?

2ND COUSIN. Garden.

1ST COUSIN. Priest in the garden?

2ND COUSIN. Book. Crucifix.

1ST COUSIN. Carrying a book and a crucifix? (*A pause. To* FULBERT.) He's married her.

FULBERT. What do you mean?

1ST COUSIN. He's sneaked into your house and married her.

FULBERT. Married? Here? Not in church?

1ST COUSIN. Down there. In your garden. On the compost heap.

2ND COUSIN. Compost heap.

ABELARD *and* HELOISE *enter.*

1ST COUSIN. Where you been hiding?

ABELARD. We walked in the street, to collect ourselves.

2ND COUSIN (*nastily*). In the street.

A pause.

ABELARD. Canon…

FULBERT (*interrupting*). What have you done in my house, in the middle of the night?

ABELARD. I have married your niece, Canon.

1ST COUSIN. On the compost.

2ND COUSIN. Compost.

ABELARD. In the garden yes, under God's sky.

1ST COUSIN. With the devil's worms.

2ND COUSIN. Worms.

ABELARD (*to* FULBERT, *trying to ignore the* COUSINS).
This settles what was between us. I've done what I promised.

FULBERT. But why like this? As if you were stealing the holy
sacrament of matrimony, like thieves?

ABELARD. We want your blessing.

HELOISE. Please, Uncle, understand us, we need your blessing.

FULBERT *stares at him.* ABELARD *takes a breath.*

ABELARD. All we ask, is that our marriage be kept secret.

A silence.

FULBERT. Secret? Why?

1ST COUSIN. Why?

2ND COUSIN. Why?

FULBERT. Is marriage something filthy to you, that you want
to keep from the world? Do you think I'm a fool, who will
keep silent? Say to myself 'Everyone thinks Abelard comes
to my house to have my girl like a common prostitute…'

1ST COUSIN. Prostitute, that's right!

2ND COUSIN. Prostitute!

HELOISE (*low*). Peter, let's leave.

FULBERT. But secretly, I know it's all right. But I can't say.
Cos it's a secret. I can smile at all the people in the
congregation in Notre Dame, and say to myself you all think
I'm a Pandar, a bawd, servicing my niece to the great
Abelard… But secretly, all is well! The world is all to rights
though the world does not know it!

HELOISE (*increasingly frightened*). Peter…

FULBERT. You are both so educated, subtle, clever. All that
learning, philosophy, why do you use it to do this to me?
(*The anger floods back.*) I will not bear it! You insult me!
I will have recompense!

1ST COUSIN. Revenge!

2ND COUSIN. Revenge!

The 1ST COUSIN *cracks the whip down upon the stage. A loud crack.*

ABELARD (*to* HELOISE). Go to my lodgings. Now.

1ST COUSIN. Stay where you are!

ABELARD. She is my wife, she is leaving this house.

1ST COUSIN. I say strip them!

2ND COUSIN. Strip!

1ST COUSIN. Tie them together! Flay the skin off them!

2ND COUSIN. Skin off!

The 1ST COUSIN *cracks the whip on the stage again.* HELOISE *and* ABELARD *huddle together.* FULBERT *falls to his knees, in great distress.*

FULBERT. Leave. Before I do such a thing to you. Leave.

HELOISE. Uncle...

Exit FULBERT. *The* 1ST COUSIN *cracks the whip onto the stage, twice, and exits.*

Where can we go?

ABELARD. Mother Helene. I trust her.

HELOISE. You mean –

ABELARD *takes her by the hand and they run off.*

Scene Three

Convent. MOTHER HELENE, HELOISE, *dressed as a nun, and* ABELARD, *who wears a cloak.*

HELENE. You are welcome to the convent of Ste Marie Argenteuil.

HELOISE. Thank you, Mother.

She bows.

HELENE. I have asked the novices to prepare two guest rooms for you. They are not remotely near each other.

ABELARD. Helene. We are married.

HELENE. I know of the events of the night before last.

ABELARD. Can news travel that fast?

HELENE. About France's favourite lovers? And with the enemies you have?

ABELARD (*smiling at* HELOISE). We don't understand the effect our few kisses have had, my dear.

HELENE (*unsmiling*). You certainly do not. (*Turning away.*) I will have food brought to your rooms.

HELOISE. Oh, can't we eat in the refectory? This is my old house, I went to school here. I would be so happy, to eat with the sisters and their pupils.

HELENE. It is better that you eat in your rooms.

HELOISE. Why? (*Realises.*) Oh. That makes me feel... dirty. Do you want me to feel dirty here?

HELENE. I have to keep discipline here, Madame Abelard, amid young women who are simple souls, and who will never know the things you have known... (*Looking at* ABELARD.) or tasted. (*Pauses. To* HELOISE.) I have to ask one thing. Why are you dressed as a bride of Christ, when you are only a bride of Adam?

ABELARD. Don't be hard on her, Helene. The habit was my idea, a ruse to get her out of the city, unseen by her uncle's drunken friends.

HELENE. No matter. Many kinds of women have worn a habit, for many reasons. But perhaps you assume the clothes of what you are not, too readily.

HELOISE (*bows her head*). I stand corrected.

HELENE. I suspect you are beyond correction. But I...

She hesitates.

HELOISE. Yes, Mother?

HELENE (*unable to look at* HELOISE). I admire you. For what you have tried to be. And I pray for you.

HELENE *exits, quickly.*

HELOISE. Oph! I thought she was going to eat me alive. Then she says that.

ABELARD *is about to speak but three young* NUNS *enter –* BERTHODE, FRANCINE *and* MARIE. *They go straight to* HELOISE *and* ABELARD. *The* NUNS *keep their eyes focused on the ground.*

BERTHODE (*to* HELOISE). Please come with us.

FRANCINE (*to* ABELARD). Please come with us.

The two groups cross. ABELARD *manages to say to* HELOISE...

ABELARD. One hour's time. In the chapel.

HELENE *enters. She kneels and prays.*

HELENE. Omnipotens et misericors Deus, qui propter eximiam caritatem tuam, qua dilexisti nos, Filium tuum unigentitum, Dominum Nostrum Jesum Christum, de coelis in terram descendere, et de beatissimae Virginis Mariae Dominae nostrae utero sacratissmo... per eundem Christum Dominum nostrum. Amen.

HELENE *crosses herself, waits a moment, then stands and exits. Enter* HELOISE *and* ABELARD.

HELOISE (*whisper*). Peter?

ABELARD. Yes.

HELOISE. I thought she was never going to go! Where are you?

ABELARD. Second pillar from the back. Where are you?

HELOISE. Behind the altar. Shall I come to you, or you to me?

ABELARD. I to you.

> ABELARD *runs across the stage to behind the altar.*
> HELOISE*'s head appears.* ABELARD *kneels down with her.*
> *We see their heads behind the altar.* HELOISE *giggles. Her*
> *mood is oddly blithe.*

(*Irritated.*) What? What?

HELOISE. This is our honeymoon.

ABELARD. You will be safe here. I will go back to Paris. I will try again to smooth your uncle's mind.

HELOISE (*a giggle*). His mind does seem very wrinkled.

ABELARD. Please. We must come through this. We must have a plan.

HELOISE. Excellent and perfect master plan number two! We have no idea what to do at all, do we? (*Shouts.*) Do we!

ABELARD. Sh!

HELOISE. No idea what we're going to do in the morning, let alone for the rest of our lives. Mm? Mm?

> *A pause.*

ABELARD. Forgive me. I have been reckless.

HELOISE. I would not be with you if you were not reckless, Peter Abelard. (*A pause.*) I want to take my clothes off, then take off yours.

ABELARD. Heloise, we are behind the altar of a chapel in a convent...

HELOISE. We weren't married before an altar, but we can have our first time as man and wife on one!

ABELARD. I don't know if this is the idea we need at this moment...

HELOISE. We mean nothing impure. And all that matters, is the purity of intent. No, my loving husband?

The NUNS *enter,* BERTHODE *encountering the others.*

BERTHODE. Marie, Francine. They're in the chapel.

MARIE. Praying?

BERTHODE. Not praying.

FRANCINE. Not… Not in the chapel!

BERTHODE. I saw them through the gap in the door. Where we peek sometimes, when Mother is in there alone, crying.

MARIE. Yes yes, tell us.

BERTHODE. First, I saw her. She stood up behind the altar, and lifted off her habit. She had nothing on underneath.

FRANCINE. Oh.

MARIE. Oh dear.

BERTHODE. No shift, nothing. She stood there. In the moonlight, her body was bluey gray. So beautiful. He was kneeling before her. She leant over him, and kissed him on the mouth.

FRANCINE. Oh.

MARIE. Unbearable.

BERTHODE. Then she lifted his clothes from him, and he stood up, in the bluey-gray light from the window, naked as he was born. And she called him husband, and he called her wife. And they embraced.

FRANCINE. Oh no.

MARIE. No.

BERTHODE. And he told her that he would love her till death. And she threw herself back in his arms, leaning back, her hair streaming behind her, as if she had abandoned herself, and she laughed.

MARIE. Threw herself back… What, like this?

MARIE *embraces* FRANCINE *and leans back with the movement we have seen* HELOISE *make, embracing* ABELARD.

BERTHODE. And then she lifted herself upon him, with her legs up around his back, and she took a great breath, and made a strange, sharp cry…

MARIE *jumps up in* FRANCINE*'s arms and twines her legs behind her back. She makes a cry. But* FRANCINE *cannot hold her.* BERTHODE *comes to their aid. All three fall to the ground and roll over in a heap, laughing. They calm down.* BERTHODE *continues.*

And then she pulled herself round, and she leaned back, and pulled him down upon her, and he climbed up upon the holy altar.

FRANCINE. On the altar?

MARIE. Please not.

BERTHODE. And so they accepted each other, as the lovers they are.

A silence. She jumps up.

Shall we go and look? Come on!

ABELARD *and* HELOISE *slip up onto the altar and fall asleep.*

MARIE. It will be matins soon, shouldn't we wake them? We could make a little noise, at the back…

BERTHODE. Not just yet. Let's look at them, for a little while.

BERTHODE *kneels before them. Then the other two kneel.*

Scene Four

ABELARD*'s lodgings.*

Six MEN, *their faces variously covered by masks, scarves and hoods, have forced their way into the room.* FULBERT *and the* 1ST *and* 2ND COUSIN *are among them, but* FULBERT*'s presence is not apparent until the end of the scene.* ABELARD *confronts them. He is wearing a white nightshirt.*

ABELARD. Who are you?

1ST COUSIN. We're farmers.

2ND COUSIN. Farmers.

ABELARD. What is this nonsense? What do you mean, bursting into my lodgings in the middle of the night? Get out.

1ST COUSIN. We told you! We're farmers, come to do farmer's work!

2ND COUSIN. Farmer's work!

1ST COUSIN. The bull that gets into the cows, Abelard. The bull that humps everything, kicks over fences, that gets too juicy for his own good...

2ND COUSIN. Juicy!

1ST COUSIN. How do you quiet him down, eh? Eh?

ABELARD (*takes a step back*). Gentlemen, you have me at a disadvantage.

1ST MAN. If thine eye offend thee...

2ND MAN....pluck it out!

1ST MAN. If a thing on a man offend thee...

2ND MAN....cut it off!

They rush at ABELARD, *with a roar, and pull him down onto the floor. He disappears beneath them.*

1ST COUSIN. Doing nothing illegal here!

1ST MAN. It's in the law!

2ND COUSIN. Fulbert has witnesses in the family!

2ND MAN. He has the right!

ABELARD. Please! We are in France! A civilised country!

2ND COUSIN. Farming country!

> *Out of the scrum of* MEN *pinning* ABELARD *down, an arm is raised, wielding a large knife. It glints.*

1ST MAN. We do this in the name of outraged Christian French womanhood.

2ND MAN. Your bull days are done.

2ND COUSIN. Bull days done.

1ST COUSIN. You'll be a different animal now.

> *The knife disappears.* ABELARD *screams and at once the group of* MEN *scatters.* ABELARD's *white nightshirt is soaked in blood about his groin. He begins to slowly drag himself away upstage.* FULBERT *pulls his hood back. He is in shock.*

There you are cousin. Recompense.

> *He hands something bloody to* FULBERT, *who looks at what he is holding. He opens his mouth in horror and looks up. The other* MEN *drag him away and exit, running.* ABELARD *continues to drag himself upstage.*

Scene Five

ABELARD *is dragging himself away.*

The Convent of Ste Marie Argenteuil.

The young NUNS *enter, running.*

FRANCINE. But what have they done?

MARIE. It was three nights ago. A monk brought a message from the Abbey of St Denis.

BERTHODE. It's a terrible lover's fate. Like Tristan and Iseult.

FRANCINE. It's not fate, it's just horrible.

MARIE. The worst thing in the world.

FRANCINE. But what is 'emasculated'? (*Realises.*) Oh. Like horses. Oh.

   MOTHER HELENE *enters.*

HELENE. All of you. Go to the chapel at once.

ALL. Yes, Mother.

FRANCINE. Like a gelding!

HELENE. The chapel! In absolute silence!

ALL. Yes, Mother.

   The NUNS *go upstage and kneel. We hear the subdued weeping of one or two of them. Then* HELENE *enters with* HELOISE, *who is half-fainting. She falls to the floor on her hands and knees.*

HELENE. Stand up!

HELOISE. I want to die.

HELENE. You will not die. Smell this…

HELOISE. I must…

HELENE. You must smell this and stand up, that is all!

   She holds a small bundle of twigs beneath HELOISE's *nose.*

   Breathe!

HELOISE *breathes in twice. The remedy takes immediate effect. She is wide awake.*

HELOISE. I must go to him.

HELENE. You cannot.

HELOISE. Don't tell me what I can or cannot do. He is my husband. I am going to him.

HELENE. He has entered the Abbey of St Denis.

HELOISE. 'Entered'?

A pause.

HELENE. They waived the novitiate for him. He took his vows at once.

A pause.

HELOISE. Peter is a *monk*? (*Laughs. The laughter dies.*) Oh horrible, horrible.

HELENE. The brothers of the Abbey are nursing him.

HELOISE. Oh horrible, horrible.

HELENE. He is still alive. Comfort yourself in that.

HELOISE *pauses, trying to control herself, wiping her face, pulling at her clothes. She calms down.* HELENE, *also distressed, looks away during this.*

HELOISE. You have a reliable report from the Abbey?

HELENE. Yes.

HELOISE. How much pain is he in?

HELENE. I cannot hide… that he suffers, but with great courage.

HELOISE. Is the wound…

HELENE. You must take comfort. He has survived for three days. (*Hesitates.*) But I cannot hide that I was told the wound is… complete.

HELOISE (*oddly*). Complete. Com… plete. Com… plete.

HELENE. He… (*Pauses.*) Brother Abelard has sent you a message.

HELOISE *is mouthing soundlessly the words 'Total, utterly',
looking away from* HELENE.

He wishes you to take vows and enter this house as a bride
of Christ.

HELOISE *stops mouthing the words*.

The convent of Ste Marie Argenteuil will, as the Abbey did
for your husband, waive the stage of novice. You will
become a sister here, at once.

HELOISE. No.

HELENE. That is what he wishes.

HELOISE. He wants me to be a *nun*? First he wanted me to be
his wife, now he wants me to be a... *thing*? On her knees,
scrubbing floors and praying? Who only knows she is a
woman because she bleeds into rags once a month?

HELENE. You are forgetting yourself.

HELOISE. They cut his sex out! Now he wants to cut out mine!

HELENE *strikes her on the face.* HELOISE *grunts with the
shock and steps back, holding her cheek.*

HELENE. Listen. Listen to me. By becoming a sister, you
won't be leaving life, you'll be rejoining it.

HELOISE. Oh wonderful! Am I now to get the nun's sermon?

HELENE. This love affair. Do you think that was *in* life? It was
not. It knew no days, weeks, years. It existed only for itself.
When you were in each other's arms, your bodies only knew
that night, that moment. Time could not be counted by the
burning of a candle, the rising of the moon, the movement of
the stars. You and Peter weren't in real life, or real time at
all. Even as your affair happened, it was a memory. Think.
When you remember yourself with him, don't you see him
and you, from above? Your body with his, naked on a bed, or
on your clothes, strewn upon the grass?

HELOISE (*hesitates. Low*). Yes.

HELENE. How can you remember yourself out of your body?
See? Even the memory of love isn't real. It becomes just a
beautiful story. Not life.

HELOISE. How do you know, about seeing yourself...

And HELENE *is angry.*

HELENE. What a selfish, stuck-up little madam you are. Do
you think you're the only woman in the world to have been
with a man in the grass?

HELOISE *pauses.*

HELOISE. Sermon me a little more, Mother.

HELENE. You can do it for yourself. Go on!

HELOISE. My old life is dead. I must begin a new one.

HELENE (*matter of fact*). Yes.

HELOISE. And where else can I go?

HELENE. Where else?

HELOISE. Not Paris. Not Peter's family farm, when they learn
about what he wishes for me. I am a 'woman with a bad
past'. Very nunnable. Along with the second and third
daughters of families who can't sell them off to husbands.
Women who can't have a husband, except for Jesus.

HELENE. Except for Him.

HELOISE. I have no vocation, Mother.

HELENE. Yes you do. It may not be religious, for now anyway,
but your calling rages in you. I know you were happy in this
house when you were a schoolgirl. Join it now, as a teacher.

HELOISE. I cannot, not a nun's ring...

HELENE (*smiles*). The time for fucking in trees is over, my dear.

HELOISE. Is it, is it? Oh I wish, just once, I... forgive me,
Mother.

HELENE *takes her hands. A pause.*

How long will it take, before I stop loving him?

HELENE. Oh, I expect you will love him for ever, Sister Heloise.

End of Act Two.

ACT THREE

Scene One

Twenty years later.

ALBERIC *and* LOTHOLF *are on the road again to the Abbey of Clairvaux. They are both gray-haired.* LOTHOLF *looks prosperous.* ALBERIC, *wearing ecclesiastical dress, is all but a cripple and has constant pain, walking with two custom-made crutches that are tied to his arms.*

LOTHOLF. Every year. For twenty years. Always on foot.

ALBERIC. It cleanses us. It's a ritual.

LOTHOLF. It's ridiculous.

> ALBERIC *rests, wincing.*

> You are a bishop! You live in a palace! I own half the taverns in Paris and I am *very, very rich*! I do not have to do this.

ALBERIC. I am a bishop and you are rich because we are the servants of Bernard of Clairvaux, and the servants of Bernard of Clairvaux do this! (*His back spasms. Screams.*) Ah!

> *A Cistercian* MONK *runs on. He is mad.*

MAD MONK. Burning bush! Woman's bush! Fire between her legs! Guinivere, Iseult, Heloise!

> *He exits running.*

LOTHOLF (*sighs*). Nothing changes.

ALBERIC. Some things do. Didn't you hear what he said?

LOTHOLF. Just mouldy-bread madness.

ALBERIC. The names of women famous for love. The last was Heloise.

> *A* 2ND MONK *runs on. He too is mad.*

2ND MONK (*to* ALBERIC). Hey! You!

ALBERIC. What?

2ND MONK. What's doubly round and gone to Heaven?

LOTHOLF. Abelard's balls.

2ND MONK (*backing away, furious*). You've heard it! You've heard it! You've heard it!

The 2ND MONK *exits.*

ALBERIC. Is it a sign?

LOTHOLF. What do you mean?

ALBERIC. The Clairvaux lunatics, saying those names.

LOTHOLF. I hear those names all the time. Singers with trashy songs. Half the whores I run call themselves Heloise.

ALBERIC. No, it's a sign.

LOTHOLF. Nothing's a sign of anything. That's my experience. Things are just… what they are.

And they see the Abbey.

My God. There're thousands. All round the Abbey.

ALBERIC. Listen!

LOTHOLF. What?

A pause.

ALBERIC. They're all silent.

BERNARD *enters. Two* MONKS, *their faces lowered, are at his side.* ALBERIC *and* LOTHOLF *look at him.* BERNARD *does not move. His hair is grayer, but otherwise he looks the same.*

LOTHOLF. He's not going to do the feet thing again, is he? My feet haven't been bad for years. Why doesn't he do your back?

ALBERIC. Because your feet are now part of Bernard's official life story. My back is not. Saints have to do miracles. In the future, the curing of your feet could be one of the miracles that confirms Bernard in his sainthood.

LOTHOLF. But he didn't cure them. He just licked them.

ALBERIC. You have no idea that you live in a mythic time, do you?

BERNARD. My little ones.

BERNARD *and the two* MONKS *approach. He kneels down before* LOTHOLF.

LOTHOLF. Oh God.

LOTHOLF *sits down and offers his feet.* BERNARD *undoes a shoe. The* MONKS *and* ALBERIC *kneel in obsequious piety, hands together.* BERNARD *licks* LOTHOLF*'s feet. But then, to* ALBERIC *and* LOTHOLF*'s surprise, he stands abruptly, waving away the two* MONKS. *The* MONKS *exit quickly and* LOTHOLF *begins to pull his shoes back on.*

BERNARD. I must talk to you here. In the open. Even Clairvaux now has ears in the walls. Ears that listen for the eunuch.

ALBERIC *and* LOTHOLF *look at each other.*

Oh, he waxes, his obscenity grows so powerful. We had him burn his book on the Trinity. By his own hand. Before all the bishops of France. And still the book exists.

ALBERIC. Abelard had copies…

BERNARD. The Eunuch is his name. The Unclean. The Abomination.

ALBERIC. The Abomination had copies made.

BERNARD. Copies of his books, everywhere. The filthy fruit of his mutilated mind and body. The filthy book *Yes and No*, the filthy book *Theologia*, the filthy book *Conversations with a Christian and a Jew*, the filthy book *Know Thyself*. He, in his state, has the audacity to write a book called *Know Thyself*!

ALBERIC. My agents do what they can, take books out of libraries, threaten students, but his work is not universally banned by the church…

But BERNARD *is not listening.*

BERNARD. Deuteronomy chapter thirteen, verse one: 'No man whose testicles have been crushed or whose organ has been severed shall become a member of the assembly of the Lord.'

BERNARD storms away and stands with his back to them, his hands pressing the sides of his head as if with a headache.

ALBERIC. He has put the present Pope into the Vatican. He has opened sixty-eight other monasteries. He is the most powerful force in Christendom. And still it is all Abelard, Abelard.

LOTHOLF. Maybe that was the sign. He's madder than his own monks.

ALBERIC. Never say that of him! Never!

LOTHOLF. All right!

ALBERIC. Never! He has been my saviour. The mother of my soul.

LOTHOLF. Right.

He blows out air. BERNARD runs to them, at speed. Then he pauses for a moment.

BERNARD. All the books of the Abomination will be burnt. I have written to the Pope, denouncing their heresy. The Abomination has heard of my letter. He has written to me, challenging me to a disputation. At the Council of all the Church of France, in the diocese of Sens, called to take place before the King upon the first Sunday after Whitsun. (*Pauses.*) I will accept.

ALBERIC struggles to his feet.

ALBERIC. If you argue, in public, with Ab… with the Abomination, you will lose.

BERNARD looks at ALBERIC, watery-eyed.

BERNARD. Little ones, I want you to be busy. Bishop Alberic, in the days before the Council, whisper in the ears of waverers. Remind people of their loyalties. Friend Lotholf, you have a new tavern at Sens?

LOTHOLF (*surprised* BERNARD *should know this*). Yes. I do.

BERNARD. Perhaps, the Saturday before the first Sunday after Whitsun, you will invite the weaker brethren of the Council to supper.

LOTHOLF. Get them hungover, you mean. You're a deep man, Abbot.

BERNARD. Our Lord was not ashamed to appeal to publicans and sinners.

ALBERIC. Abbot Bernard, I must say this. He is heretical, but the greatest scholar in Europe. The years of suffering have honed his mind. Dispute with Abelard and you will lose.

A silence.

BERNARD. Jesus will tell me what to say.

He turns and walks away.

Scene Two

Outside the Paraclete.

BERTHODE, FRANCINE *and* MARIE – *who are agelessly young – are carrying two long beams of freshly-sawn wood across the stage, staggering under their loads. They are laughing.*

BERTHODE. It can't rain!

FRANCINE. We prayed so it won't. So it's going to be a lovely day.

MARIE. What Mother Abbess calls 'realistic prayer' – praying it won't rain when it's sunny.

They laugh.

BERTHODE. These are too heavy, let's run with them! Go!

They exit, running.

A pause, the stage empty.

DENISE *enters. She has aged. She stands still for a moment. The three* NUNS *run back on, without the wooden beams.*

 That was the last of the roof beams, sister.

DENISE. Good. Now we'd better move the thatching up from the gate. I'm worried it's green. (*Moving.*) We'll lay it out to dry, since everyone says it's going to be warm.

They all exit.

A pause, the stage empty.

Then HELOISE *enters. She is much as before, but she stands more four-square. Her girlishness is long gone. She is walking to and fro with a much aged* HELENE, *who holds* HELOISE's *arm.* HELOISE *is reading from a book. For a moment, we don't hear the text.* HELOISE *turns a page and reads.*

HELOISE. 'She takes him in her arms and then, lying at full length, she kisses his face and lips and clasps him tightly to her. Then, straining body to body, mouth to mouth, she at once renders up her spirit and, of sorrow for her lover, dies thus at his side.'

They look at each other. HELOISE *laughs and there is half a smile on* HELENE's *face.* ABELARD *enters. They do not see him. He is stiffer, he holds his body very upright. His manner is grander than it used to be.*

ABELARD. Good morning, Abbess Heloise.

HELOISE *and* HELENE *turn.*

A pause.

HELOISE. Good morning, Abbot Peter.

ABELARD (*laughs*). Extraordinary. We see each other every… five years? And we say 'good morning' as if we'd been talking the day before.

HELOISE (*straight-faced*). Perhaps we have, at last, reached some kind of understanding between us, Abbot.

ABELARD. That would be disappointing.

HELOISE. Yes, wouldn't it.

They look at each other keenly.

A pause.

Then together they realise they have ignored HELENE.

Oh, I've not told you…

ABELARD (*smiles*). Forgive me, I didn't know you'd joined Abbess Heloise here. Are you well?

HELENE *cannot speak.* HELOISE *shakes her head to* ABELARD. *He takes* HELENE*'s hand and kisses her ring.*

Mother, it is a joy in Christ to see you. The Abbess and I will always be in your debt.

HELENE *raises her hand and touches* ABELARD*'s cheek. The three of them are still for a moment.*

Then DENISE *and the three* NUNS *enter, carrying big bundles of thatching. They see* ABELARD *and stop.*

DENISE. Peter.

ABELARD. Good morning, Denise.

NUNS (*kneeling, raggedly*). Abbot… Abbot Peter…

ABELARD. No no no. This bobbing up and down, even to one low on the Ecclesiastical ladder, is a bad thing.

The NUNS *giggle.* HELOISE *does not look pleased at* ABELARD*'s pompous tone. He notices nothing.*

You are repairing the roof of the Paraclete?

DENISE. Completely replacing it.

ABELARD. It can't be in too bad a condition.

DENISE. Why, because you built it, brother?

The NUNS *are enjoying this.* HELOISE *is watchful.*

ABELARD. Built it to last, I would say.

DENISE. That was twenty years ago. Not even a roof built by Aristotle could withstand the ravages of a stone marten.

ABELARD. You had a stone marten in the attics?

DENISE. A whole family. I set a trap. But it was wrecked up there. So we thought we'd have a new roof.

ABELARD. Well! (*To the* NUNS.) Raise high the roof beam, carpenters.

A pause. DENISE is staring at ABELARD, *who does not know how to respond.* HELOISE *intervenes.*

HELOISE. Sister Denise, help Mother Helene.

DENISE. Yes, Abbess.

DENISE, HELENE and the NUNS *exit.*

ABELARD. What are you reading?

She does not move. He takes the book from her hands.

Thomas's *Tristan*? (*Laughs.*) A trashy love story? Strange devotions at the Paraclete? Though I must admit the brothers in my care have a copy.

HELOISE. Which you have read.

ABELARD. Perhaps. What's the matter with Denise?

HELOISE. Discontent amongst a body of women living together is like the weather.

ABELARD. I don't want discontent in the Paraclete.

HELOISE. Even in an abbey you have founded, there will be the occasional squall.

ABELARD. I don't want my own sister to be unhappy with you.

HELOISE. Has your philosophical work reached such a high level of complexity that you can no longer see the obvious?

A silence.

ABELARD. The boy is a man now.

HELOISE. A monk man.

ABELARD. He is at Cluny. Where I wish him to be.

HELOISE. Denise brought him up.

ABELARD. Cluny is a great house. He will be happy there.

HELOISE. Astralabe was…

ABELARD. The son to her that he never was to you or me?

HELOISE. Yes.

ABELARD. I will not speak of this any more.

HELOISE. Oh that's logical, that's dialectical. You will not speak of it because you have nothing to say about it. Do you!

ABELARD. Do you?

HELOISE. No. We both abandoned him.

ABELARD. Well, there we are then! (*Pauses.*) My God. Are we arguing like a married couple?

HELOISE. Don't we always?

ABELARD. Well! (*Laughs.*) You can't survive as a castrato, if you don't have *some* sense of the ridiculous.

HELOISE *does not reply.*

A pause.

It doesn't die.

HELOISE. Don't.

ABELARD. The body remembers.

HELOISE (*calls out*). Sister Denise! Come! At once!

ABELARD (*low*). Oh, my dear.

DENISE *enters*. ABELARD *is at once the public man.*

Denise, I have excellent news. I wanted you to hear it from me too. (*A little pause for effect.*) I have challenged Bernard the Beast, the fantastical fanatic himself, to a disputation. Before the King at Sens on the first Sunday after Whitsun. And the crazed fool... has accepted.

HELOISE *is delighted.* DENISE *is still.*

HELOISE. Peter, that is wonderful!

ABELARD. Yes!

HELOISE. After all those years, when he swore he would never... and this is why you have come to us.

ABELARD. For your help.

HELOISE. Yes!

ABELARD. I must prepare.

HELOISE. We'll get all the books out. We'll work day and night. The sisters will help, we'll divide up into teams, we'll dig out every possible argument Bernard can use.

ABELARD. And destroy it.

HELOISE. Demolish it. Then build a new roof. Over a new building.

ABELARD. New philosophy!

HELOISE. New knowledge!

ABELARD. New faith!

HELOISE. A new age!

ABELARD. We will take the irrational, the mindlessly fanatical, the cruel, out of religion. We will give reason to the teachings of Christ's church.

HELOISE. Yes. (*A pause.*) Our time has come at last, Peter.

ABELARD. Yes. This is what our lives were for.

DENISE *is crying.* HELOISE *realises and goes to comfort her.*

HELOISE. Denise, what's the matter?

DENISE. What if Bernard wins?

Scene Three

The Council of Sens.

BERNARD *alone. He holds his head as if in agony.*

BERNARD. I am in my Gethsemane. The Pharisees plot against me. Oh my sweet Jesus, my Saviour, come to me in my hour of need.

In his mind he sees Jesus. He kneels.

Lord, what am I to do?

A pause.

Be thou clean? You spoke thus to the leper. Am I... clean? Clean of sin?

A pause.

No, I will tell no man. The Abomination that comes here today. How shall I defeat him?

A pause.

Cast the first stone? But how can I? I am a man, at fault. But you have told me I am clean of sin! Yes. I will cast the stone.

He holds his hands out.

Mother Jesus, behold thy son.

He falls to his knees and bends over, vomiting. The Council assembles around the crouched and heaving BERNARD. NUNS *enter, with their backs to us. Four* BISHOPS *with crooks, wearing mitres, enter and sit on a narrow cramped bench upstage. A pause.* LOUIS *enters. The* BISHOPS *and the* NUNS *stand and bow to him.* LOUIS *sits, then everyone else sits.* BERNARD *is still bent double. He straightens.* ABELARD *enters. He carries many books, marked with parchments. He and* BERNARD *face each other.*

A silence.

In the name of Jesus Christ our Lord, Amen.

ALL. Amen.

The BISHOPS *are all drunk and belligerent.* LOUIS *is in a filthy mood. The* NUNS *buzz with whispered malice.*

BERNARD. And in His name, I cast the first stone. (*Points at* ABELARD.) This creature before you is an agent of Antichrist, a worker for the Devil, a loathsome and convinced heretic.

Gasps. A BISHOP *belches.*

Peter Abelard, I demand that this Council condemn and damn you utterly, on eleven counts of heresy. One. That you deny the Trinity.

BISHOPS (*becoming increasingly raucous as the count goes on*). Damnamus.

BERNARD. Two. That you say the Holy Spirit is an individual spirit.

BISHOPS. Damnamus.

BERNARD. Three. That you wrote the Jews who crucified Christ were innocent because they did not know what they did.

BISHOPS. Damnamus.

BERNARD. Four. That you make void the virtues of the cross, by clever words.

BISHOPS. Damnamus.

BERNARD. Five. That you teach the miracles of our Lord are but parables and never happened.

BISHOPS. Damnamus.

BERNARD. Six. That you claim the Pagan authors are Divine.

BISHOPS. Damnamus.

BERNARD. Seven. That you put human reason above God's revelation.

BISHOPS. Damnamus.

BERNARD. Eight. That in your book on logic, you claim that Faith is a mere word, nothing else.

BISHOPS. Damnamus.

A VERY DRUNK BISHOP. Three to go!

BISHOPS *and* NUNS. Nine!

BERNARD. That you teach we can never truly know God, only language.

BISHOPS. Damnamus.

BISHOPS *and* NUNS. Ten!

BERNARD. That, by the example of your filthy life, you put profane love above that of the love of our Lord.

BISHOPS. Damnamus.

BISHOPS *and* NUNS. Eleven!

BERNARD (*ecstatic*). That... that, by these vile teachings, you seek to put man at the centre of creation. Not God.

BISHOPS. Damnamus.

There is cheering and riotous applause amongst the BISHOPS *and* NUNS. BERNARD *waits for them to quieten.*

BERNARD. I have sent these counts of heresy to His Holiness Pope Innocent in Rome, demanding that you be excommunicated from Holy Church, that your books be burnt, and that you be shut up in a monastery for the rest of your life, condemned to silence.

All of them look at ABELARD.

A very long silence.

Then ABELARD *lifts his books and parchments up and slams them down, in a rage. They scatter across the stage.*

A silence.

LOUIS. For God's sake, man, defend yourself. Refute these charges.

ABELARD *does not reply.*

What is the matter with you? Do you want these madmen, these crazed fanatics, to win?

BERNARD. Louis, beware of your intemperate tongue.

LOUIS (*angrily*). I will do what I please with my tongue. This Council is called to sit before me, not you. The King does, in name at least, run this bloody country, Abbot.

Another silence.

Peter, I appeal to you as a friend. Don't let the darkness fall on the minds of men. On all the Christian world. What of your new philosophy? All the hope, the light, the progress we prayed it would bring?

A silence. Nothing from ABELARD.

My life catches up with me. Soon I will have to do what the Kings of France always do, when they die. Have a cross of ashes spread out on the floor, lie upon it, naked, and puff! I don't want to go down upon my cross of ash, knowing that France is ruled by monks – (*Pointing at* BERNARD.) led by this man. Refute the charges, I beg you.

A NUN *giggles. A* BISHOP *yawns. Another scratches himself.*

ABELARD *turns, walks away and exits, leaving his books and parchments upon the floor. The* BISHOPS *slide off their bench and kneel. The* NUNS *do the same.* LOUIS *stands wearily, goes to* BERNARD *and kneels before him.* BERNARD *puts his hand upon* LOUIS*'s head.* LOUIS *stands.*

To the ashes.

Scene Four

A garden at the monastery of St Marcel.

ABELARD *and* BERNARD. ABELARD *is suffering from Hodgkin's disease and is feverish. He sits on a stool. They are in mid-argument.*

ABELARD. I do not wish to be an Aristotle if it cuts me off from Christ!

BERNARD. You did not say so at the Council.

ABELARD. The Council of Sens wasn't a debate, it was a trial. With the verdict already decided.

BERNARD. The Lord stopped your mouth.

ABELARD. My silence was a tactic.

BERNARD. A tactic! Ha! How like you, all worldly tactics.

ABELARD. And what was rigging the Council with drunken bishops, if not a worldly tactic?

BERNARD. Your silence was a sign from God.

> ABELARD *stands in a rage and throws his stool across the stage*. BERNARD *shows no reaction*.
>
> *A silence*.

ABELARD. So what's made you, of all people, turn up amongst the bushes?

BERNARD. I have come to be reconciled.

ABELARD. Oh! Reconciliation now, is it? After admonishment then condemnation, suddenly it's Christian love? I wonder why.

BERNARD. The Lord moved me.

ABELARD. Vatican politics moved you. Oh yes, I may be in retreat here at St Marcel, but news travels to me as fast as it does to you. The excommunication on me has been lifted, is that not so?

BERNARD (*iron-voiced*). His Holiness has been generous.

ABELARD. Can't you admit it? Even a man like Innocent the Second, the Pope you made, can be overcome by a sense of justice.

BERNARD. The excommunication on you was lifted out of pity.

> ABELARD *is taken aback*.

ABELARD. Pity?

BERNARD. The Abbot of Cluny wrote to his Holiness, telling him you were dying.

ABELARD. He did what?

BERNARD. He also told him that we would meet, and be reconciled.

ABELARD. How dare the Abbot of Cluny do that! How dare anyone intercede for me. I have never asked for favour, for pity!

BERNARD (*opens his arms*). Let us embrace, and give each other the kiss of peace.

A pause, then ABELARD *is overcome by laughter.*

ABELARD. If you call me your 'little one' I'll use a worldly tactic on you I'll regret.

Suddenly he is in physical difficulty.

Get me my stool.

BERNARD. What?

ABELARD. The stool.

BERNARD *cannot grasp what he means.*

Get me the damn stool to sit on!

BERNARD. Ah.

BERNARD *picks the stool up and sets it near* ABELARD, *who sits upon it.*

The Lord harrows you, Peter.

ABELARD. Don't worry. I'll take a little warm water and have a good vomit.

BERNARD. Your bitterness, it comes from the unhappiness of your soul. Reconcile with Christ. With me. We are both his priests.

ABELARD *puts his head in his hands.*

A long silence.

Then he rubs his face and looks up.

ABELARD. Very well. Let us reconcile.

BERNARD (*hands raised in triumph*). The Lord Jesus and all the saints and the holy prophets be praised…

ABELARD. After we have disputed the differences between us.

BERNARD *freezes.*

Why not? After all there's only one other in the garden to judge us. If I turn, will I see him by the apple tree?

BERNARD *glares.*

Shall I begin?

A curt nod from BERNARD.

In the name of the Father, the Son and the Holy Ghost, amen.

BERNARD. Amen.

A pause.

ABELARD. Let me put a question to you. If God does not exist, which of the two of us has done the greatest harm?

BERNARD *is shocked. He recoils.*

BERNARD. You are a denier! You are worse than the heretics Holy Church burnt in the south!

ABELARD. It is a *dialectical* question, to start a debate about ethics.

BERNARD. There is no faith in your ethics.

ABELARD. There are no ethics in your faith.

BERNARD. I always knew you should be walled up. Utterly silenced.

ABELARD (*calm*). Abbot, the answer to the question is that even if religion were found to be false, the harm we did preaching it would have to be forgiven. For, with all our hearts, you and I always intended only to do good. Can't we be reconciled if we simply acknowledge the purity of each other's intent?

A pause, the two men looking at each other.

BERNARD. No, no no no no. This is your doctrine of the 'ethics of intention'. It puts human conscience at the centre, not the voice of God! Cannot you see your error?

ABELARD. Cannot you see your cruelty? This staring at trees and stones, and letting young men starve and crawl round the fields of Clairvaux eating grass, stripping the white from their teeth... what way to God is that? Is your faith a living death?

BERNARD. And impregnating young women in locked rooms while teaching them Holy Scripture, and fornicating upon holy altars, is that a way to faith?

ABELARD (*suddenly desperately sick*). We must find Him within us. With all our senses. Body and mind.

BERNARD. God is dead in you, Peter.

ABELARD. Humanity is dead in you, Bernard.

A silence, with neither of them looking at each other.

Then BERNARD *turns and exits, quickly.* ABELARD, *crouched upon the stool, crosses himself.*

Amen.

Scene Five

Outside the Paraclete. Autumn. Evening. DENISE *enters. She carries an axe and has a bundle of firewood on her back.* BERTHODE, FRANCINE, MARIE *and* HELENE *enter.* HELENE *is helped by* FRANCINE.

FRANCINE. Sister Denise!

HELENE *makes a signal to* DENISE.

DENISE. What? Oh no, has he come?

FRANCINE. In the chapel...

MARIE. The brothers from St Marcel brought him, just after vespers.

DENISE. How long have they been on the road with him?

MARIE. Four days.

DENISE. Dear God.

BERTHODE. Abbess Heloise sent the brothers away. Then she carried him into the chapel, in her arms.

MARIE. We daren't go in there.

Tears amongst the NUNS.

DENISE. I'll see to it.

FRANCINE. What shall we do?

Enter HELOISE.

HELOISE. I've put his books around him. Open, like flowers. And tonight I will sleep with him.

DENISE. Heloise, that is impossible.

HELOISE. It was always impossible. Everything about us was impossible.

DENISE. My dear –

HELOISE. I am going to stay with my husband, all night.

DENISE. You can't –

HELOISE. I will lie with my husband in my arms.

DENISE. The body, there's infection –

HELOISE. I am going to stay with my husband, all night.

DENISE (*pauses, then lowers her veil. Kneeling*). Then I am going to stay with my brother, all night.

HELOISE. As you wish.

She stretches her arms and arches her back.

I think I'll go to bed now.

Scene Six

Outside the Paraclete. Winter. The NUNS *can be heard still singing in the distance. After a while,* HELOISE *enters. She is walking, reading from a small book with great concentration, mouthing words silently.* BERNARD *enters. He has a staff.*

BERNARD. Abbess Heloise.

A pause.

HELOISE. Abbot Bernard.

BERNARD. It is many years since we met.

HELOISE. You came to the Paraclete the year after it was opened, I recall. You criticised the form of certain phrases in our prayers.

BERNARD. In a brotherly way, to a sister community.

HELOISE. Indeed.

A pause.

BERNARD. I have made this journey, to console you in your grief.

A long pause.

HELOISE. That is very kind of you, Abbot. Perhaps we can offer you a meal…

BERNARD. I had my daily bread, many hours ago.

HELOISE. Some wine?

BERNARD. Nothing.

A pause. HELOISE *does not know what to say.*

HELOISE. I…

BERNARD (*interrupting*). What are your devotions, Abbess?

HELOISE. This? It's a book of Arabic grammar.

BERNARD. Arabic?

HELOISE. Peter always wanted to read the Koran. Now there is a school at Salerno, in Sicily, where they are beginning to translate Arab texts.

BERNARD (*darkly*). I have heard of the school of Salerno.

HELOISE. Some of the Arabic books they have are translations themselves. From ancient Greek. There is a rumour that they have discovered a new book by Aristotle called… *Ethics.*

BERNARD *is seething with anger.*

BERNARD. Are you unrepentant and unreformed, woman?

HELOISE. Oh absolutely. As Peter was.

BERNARD. But the Lord cut him down, eh? Hunh? Hunh. Hunh.

A silence.

HELOISE. Thank you for your consolation.

BERNARD. I do not deny your loss.

She laughs out loud at him.

Do you even laugh about the holiness of death?

HELOISE. Peter just died. And that is all there is to be said.

BERNARD. We were reconciled at the end.

HELOISE. No you weren't.

BERNARD. I visited him. We were reconciled.

HELOISE. You were not. But you will make it part of your life story. As you hope coming to console me, will be part of your life story. You are all story, Abbot. You are not really living at all.

BERNARD (*iron in his voice*). We met. We were reconciled.

A pause.

HELOISE. You've lost, you know.

BERNARD. I think not. The books of his that are not banned, are removed from the libraries. His students are scattered and discouraged. I will preach a crusade to the new King. France will burn in religious fire. All your Aristotle, your Greek 'humanism' will be smoke in the Devil's eye. And a new age of faith and obedience will dawn.

HELOISE. Ah well. (*Looks away.*) I suppose there's Peter's autobiography.

BERNARD. His what?

HELOISE. He called it *History of My Sorrows*. Peter was always a little self-dramatising.

BERNARD. Abelard wrote an autobiography? (*A dread comes over him.*) Am I in it?

HELOISE. Oh we're all in it. And there are our letters.

BERNARD. Letters? What letters?

HELOISE. Our letters.

BERNARD. You wrote letters?

HELOISE. Oh yes, full of our love and pain, and our hopes to
live a better life. There are copies translated into every
language in the world. (*Taking the Penguin paperback
edition out of her habit.*) Look, here's one in English, eight
hundred and fifty years from now.

She holds the Penguin book out to BERNARD, *who stares at
it, then out to the audience.*

Blackout.

End of play.

www.nickhernbooks.co.uk

facebook.com/nickhernbooks

twitter.com/nickhernbooks